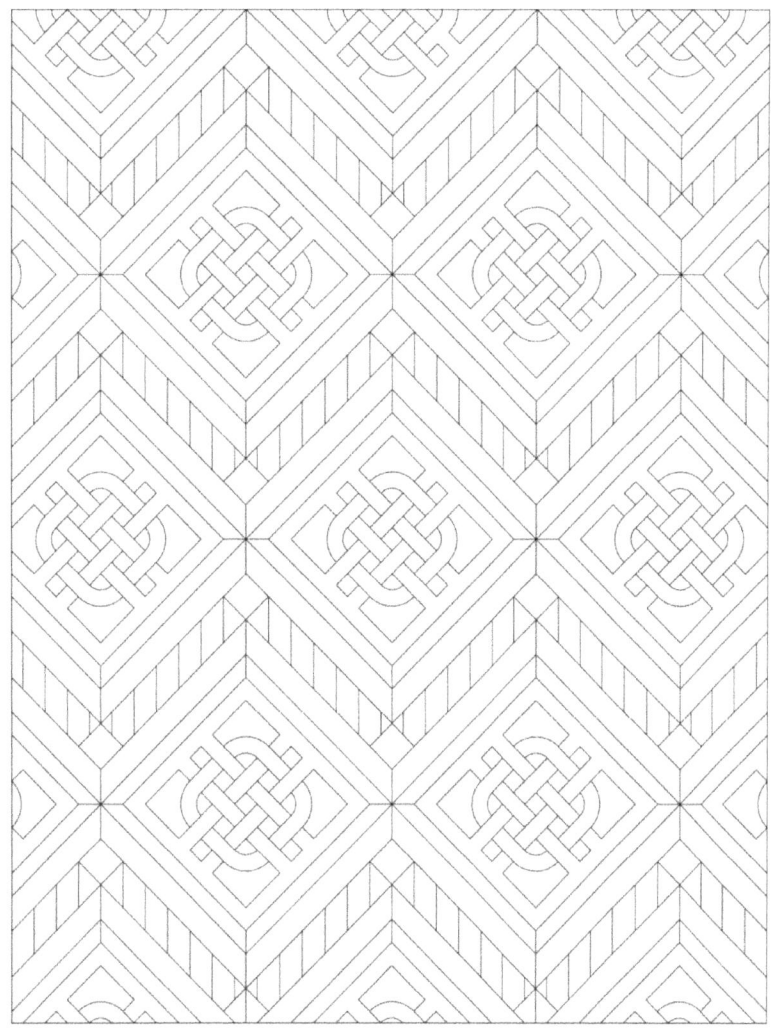

Coloring Designs 2

A Coloring Book for Grown-Ups

Colored pencils, markers, and a variety of other media are suitable for use when coloring this book. To help reduce the risk of bleed-through, please place a blank sheet of paper between the pages when coloring.

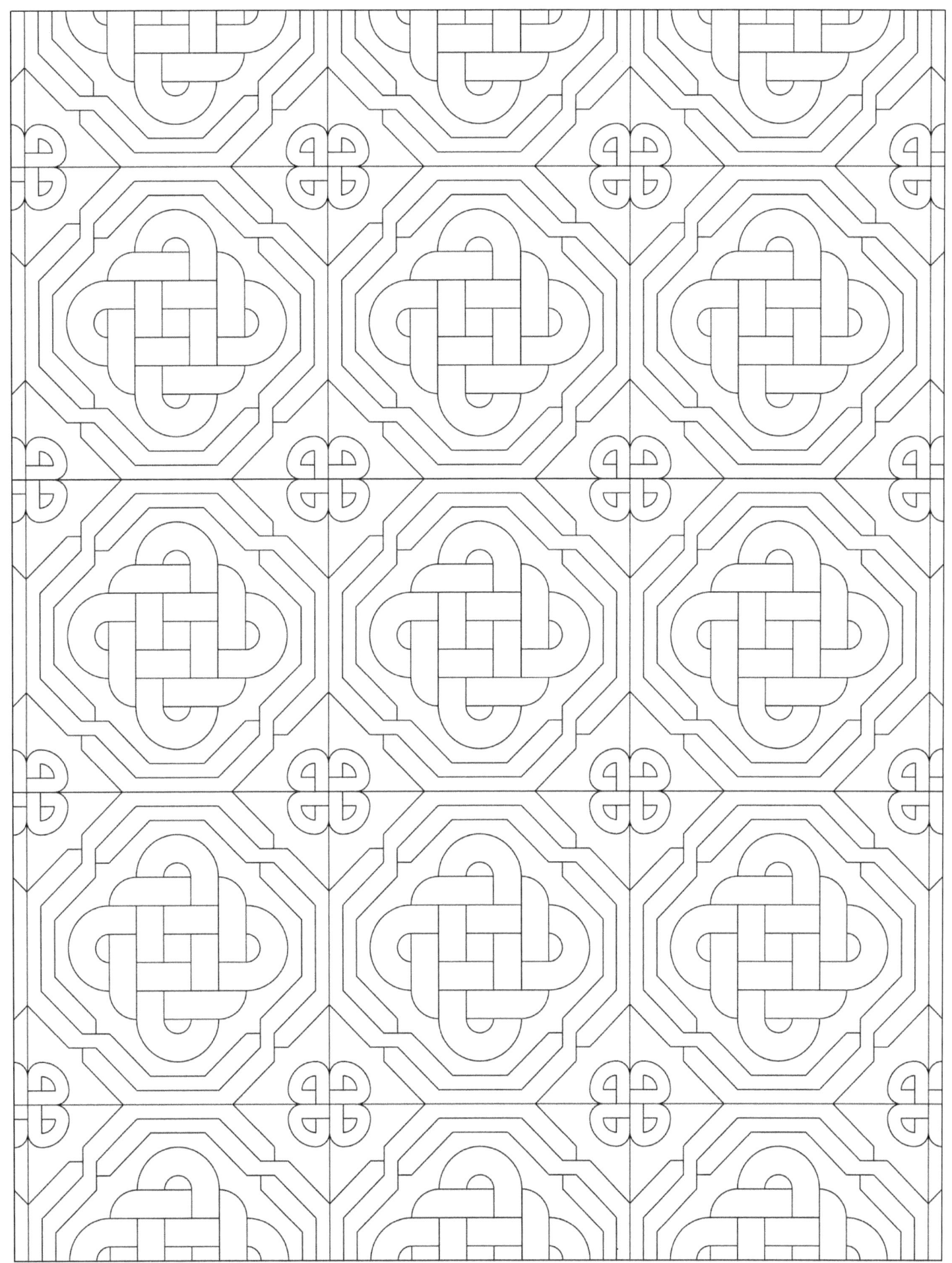

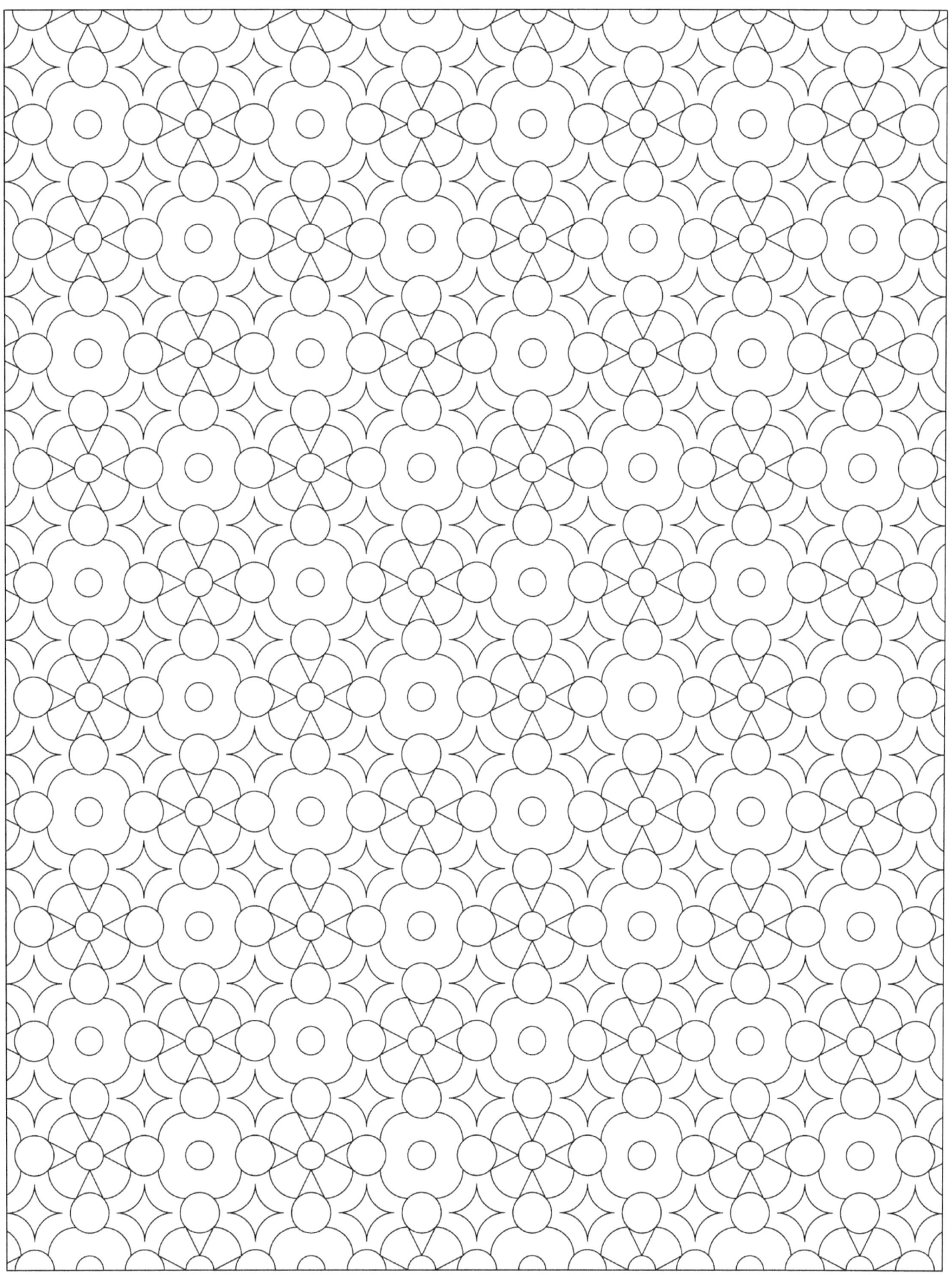

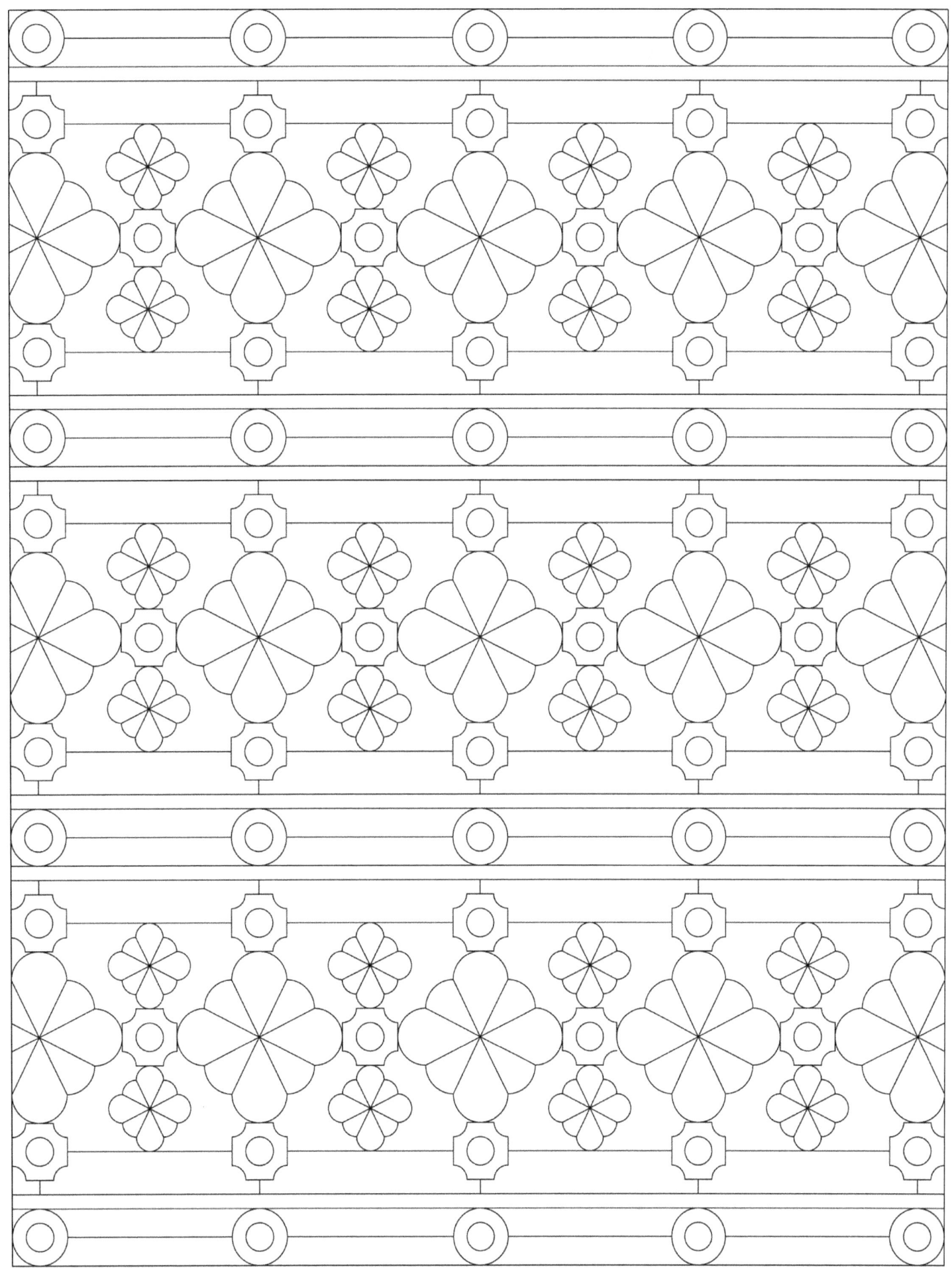

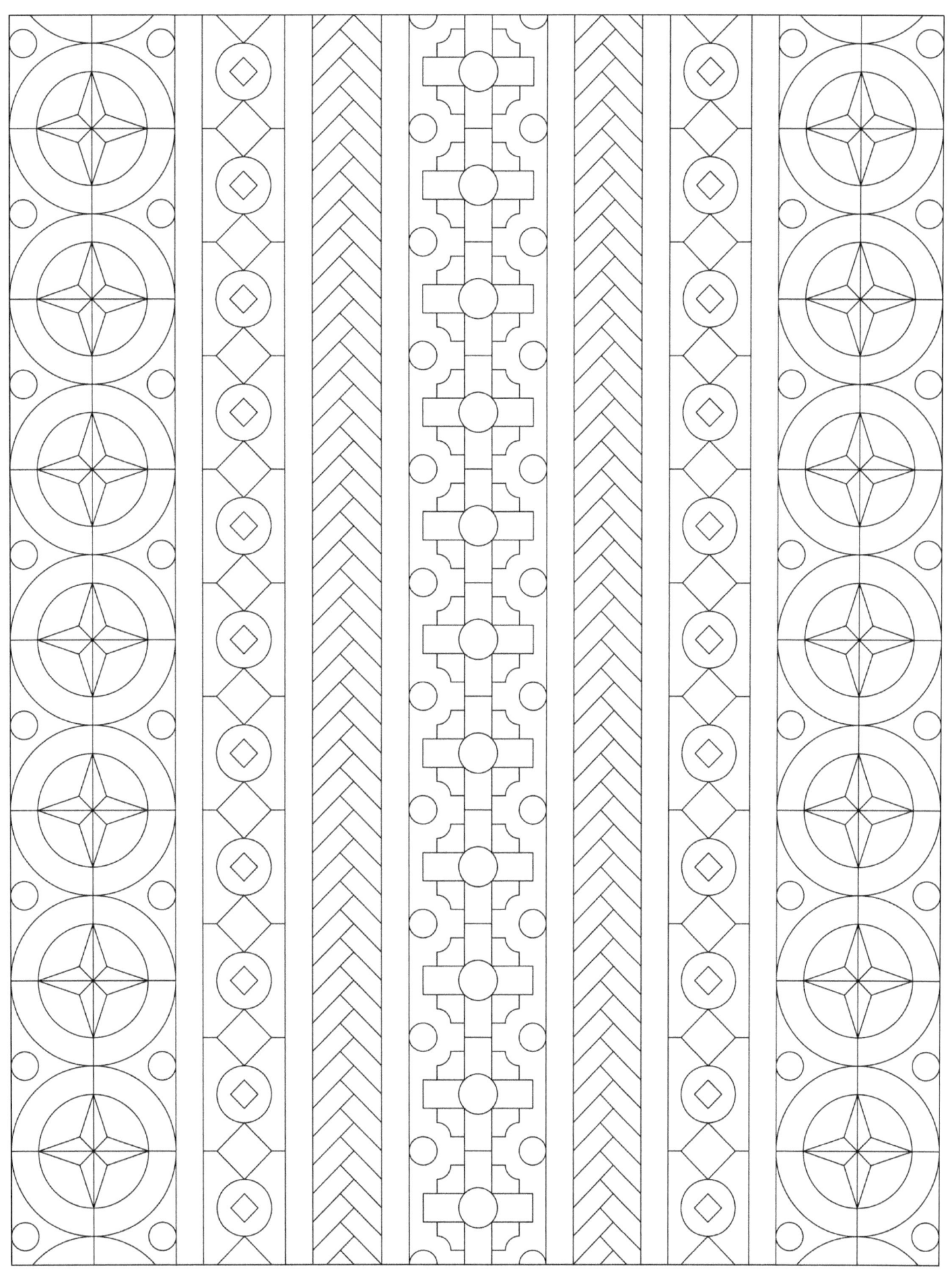

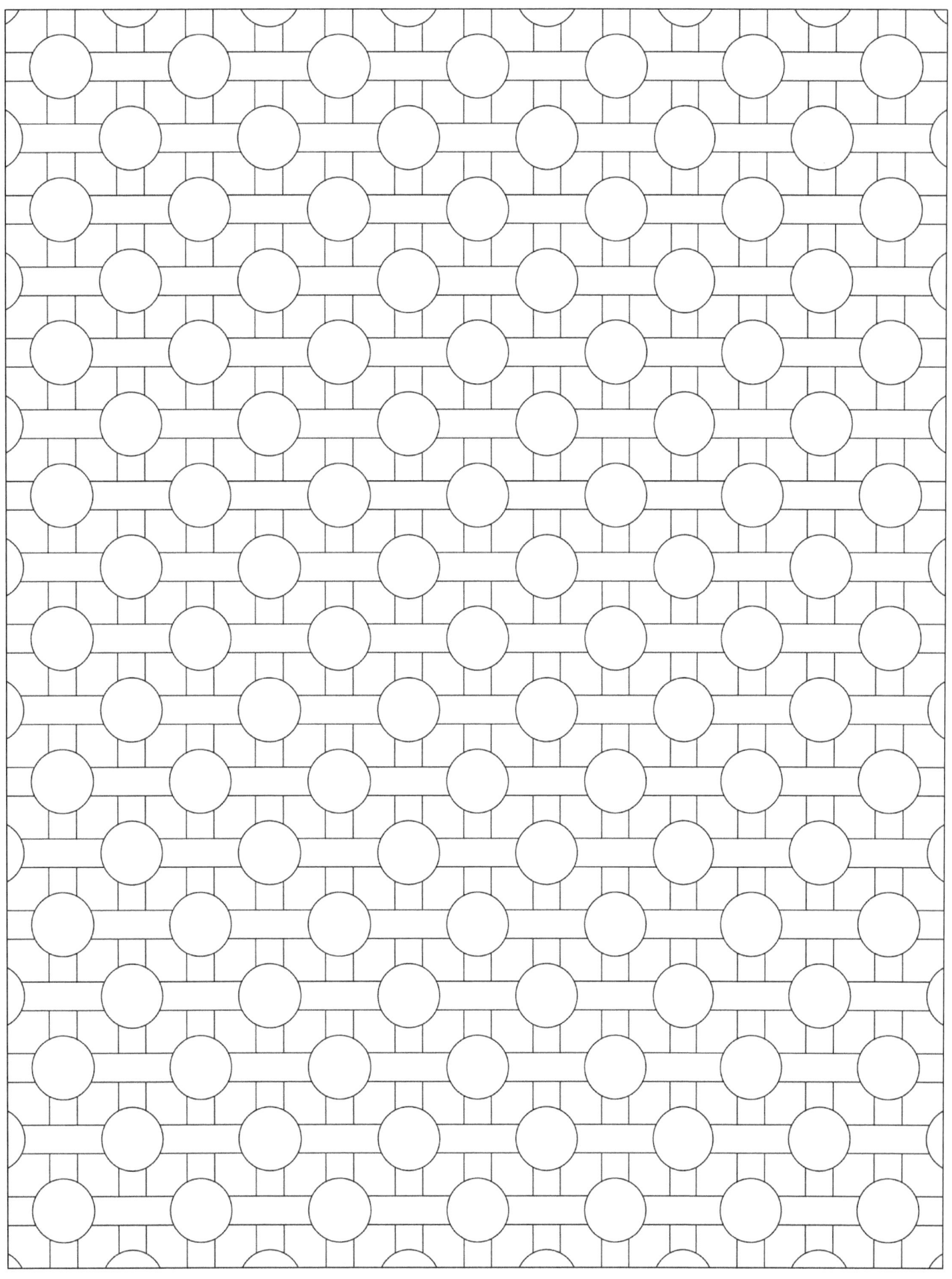

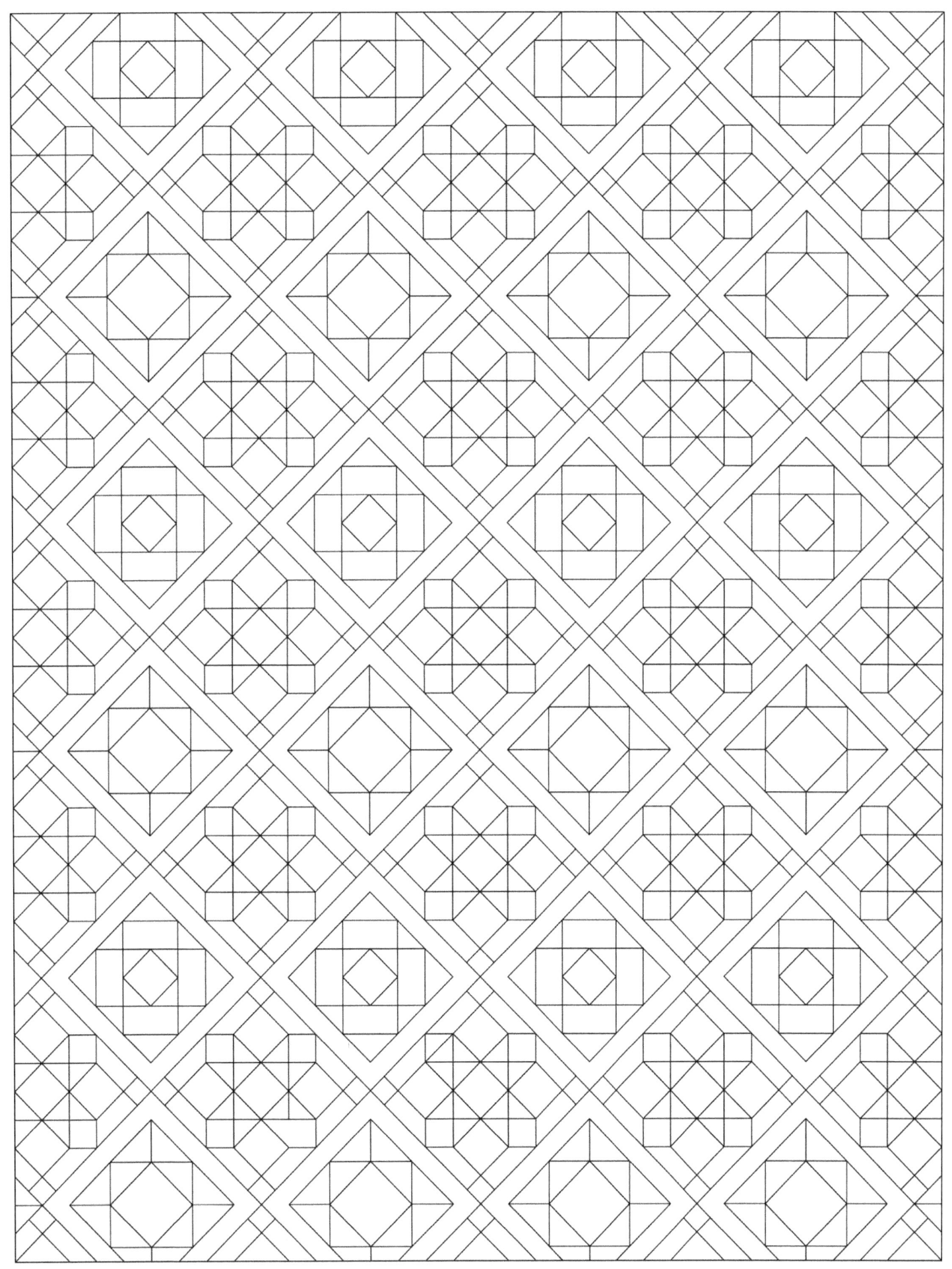

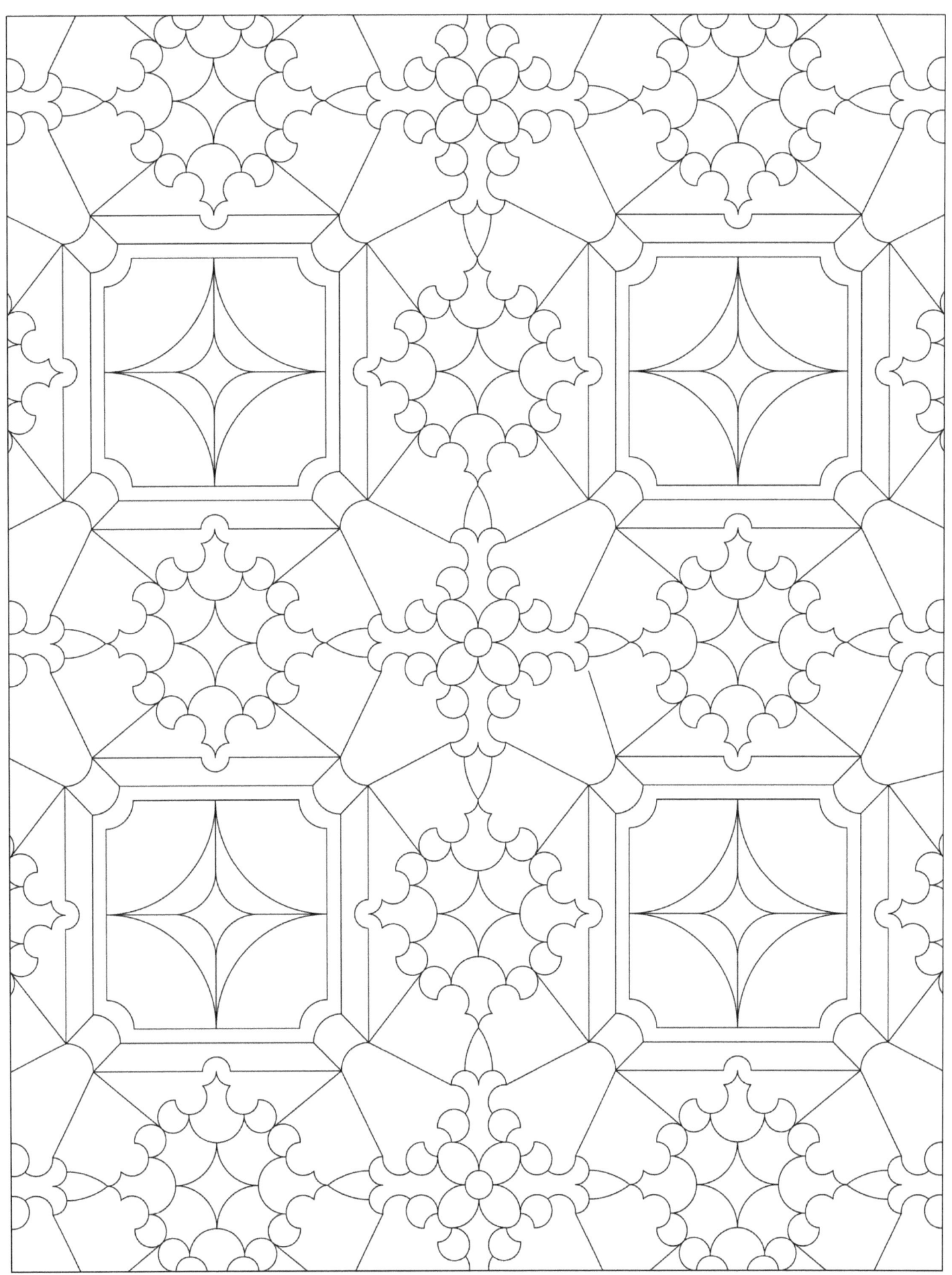

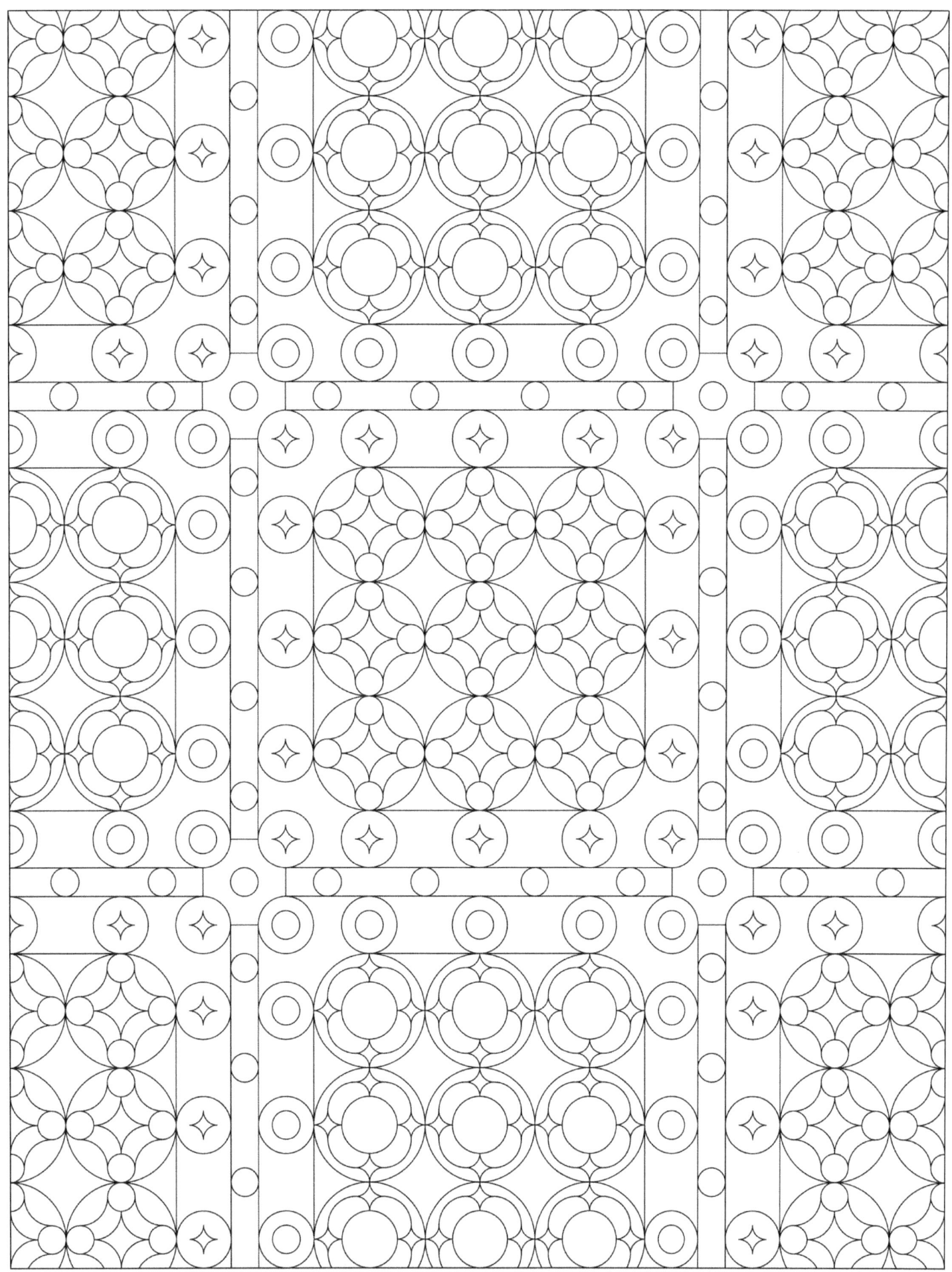

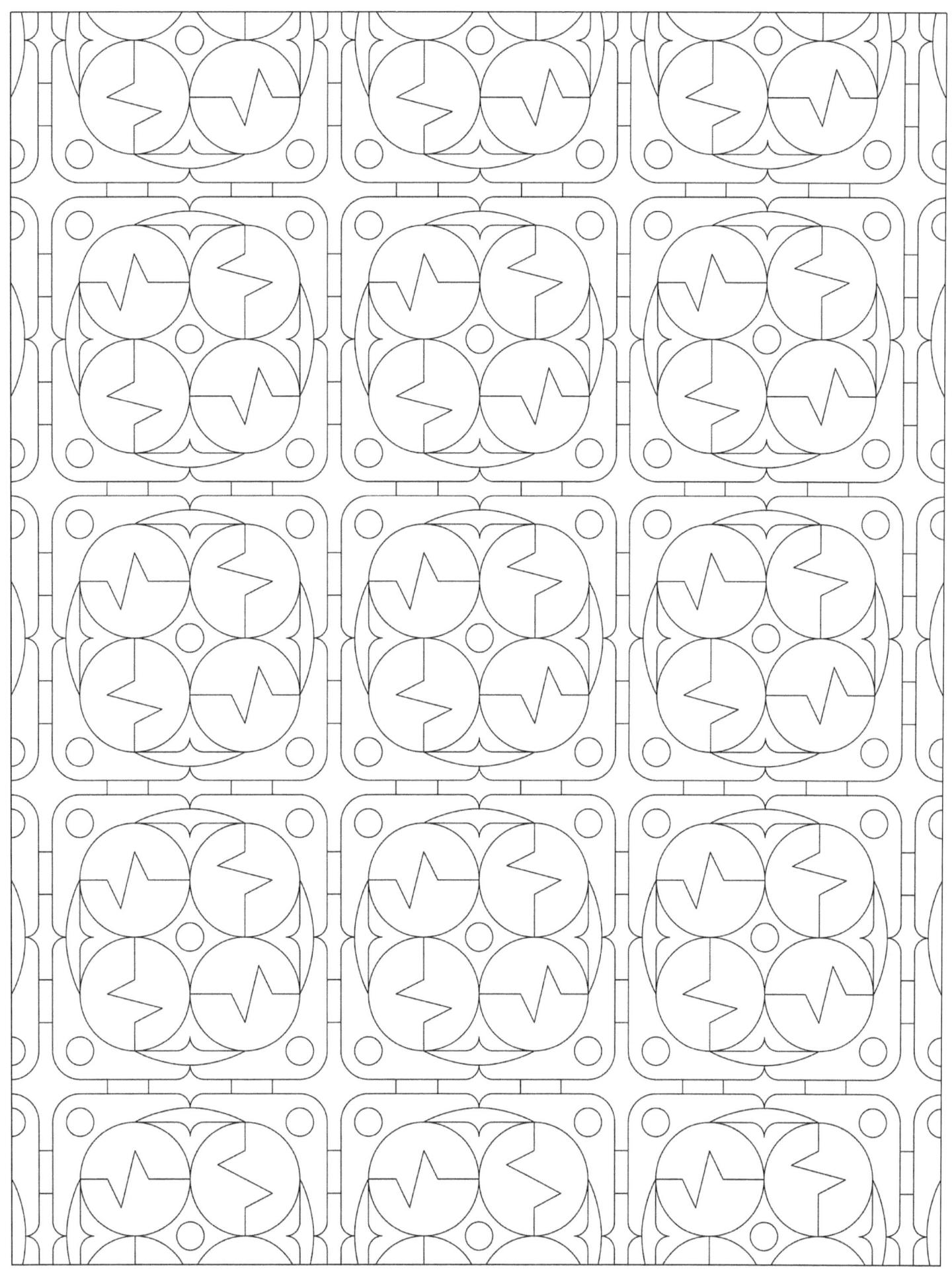

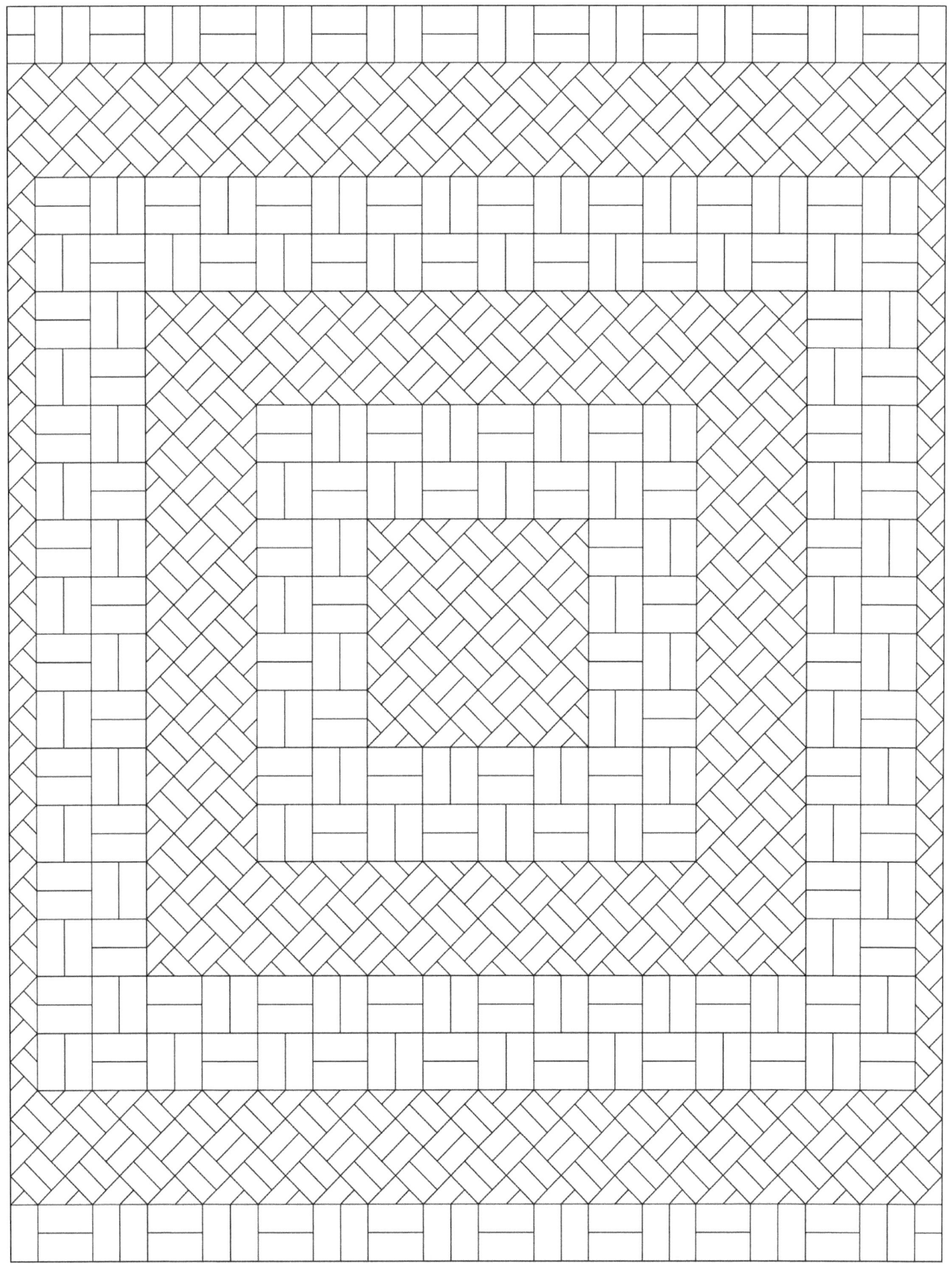

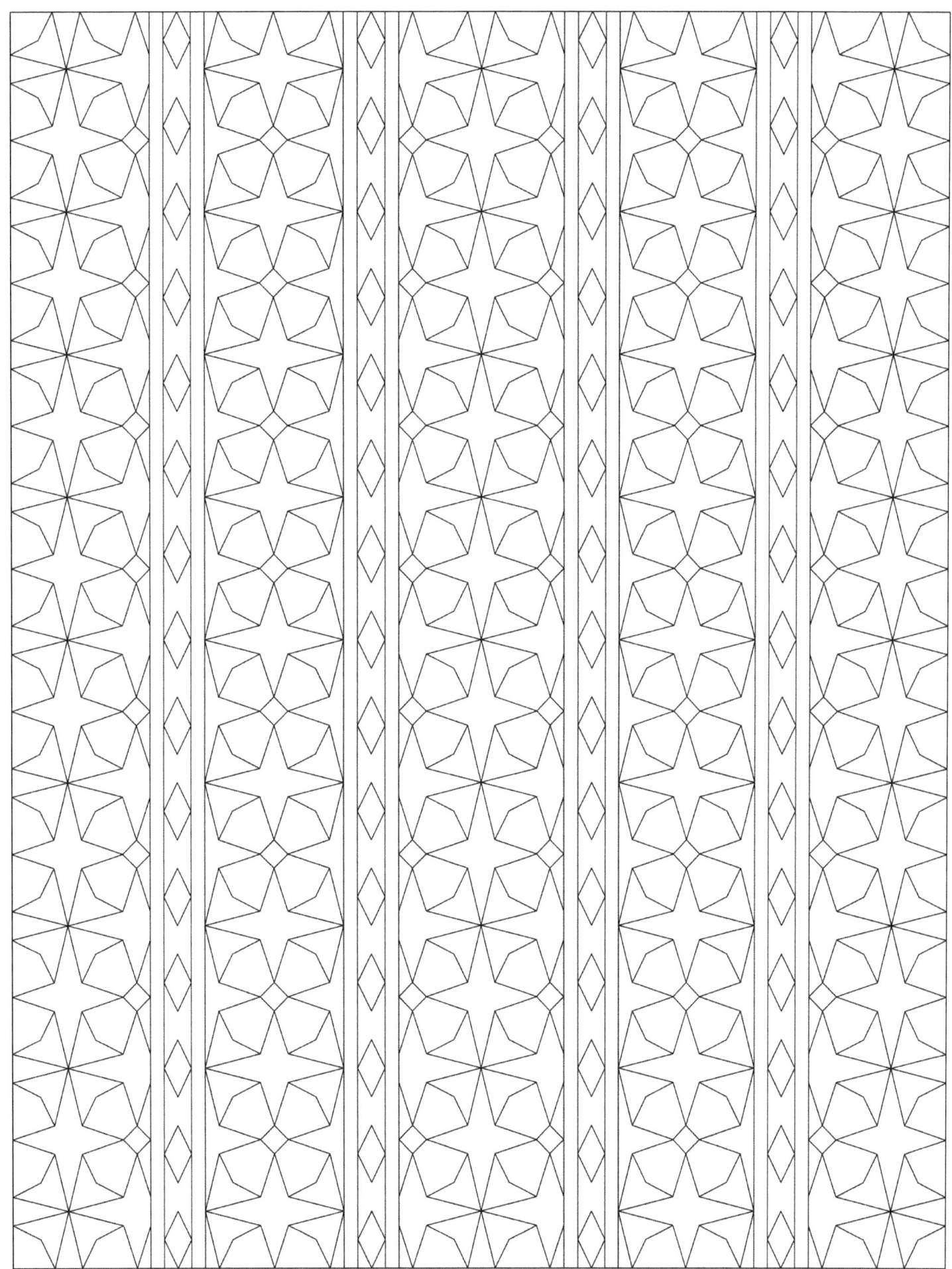

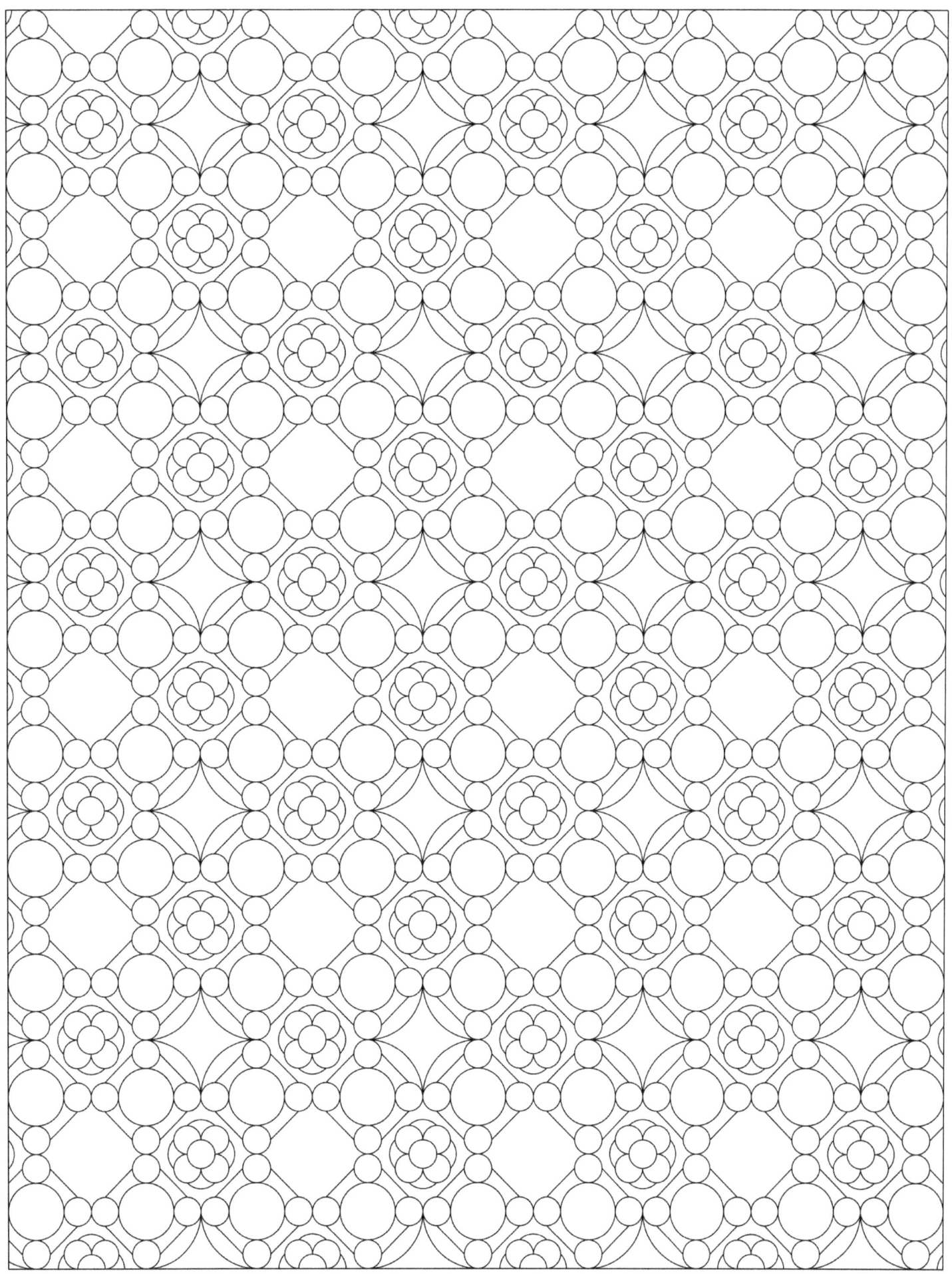

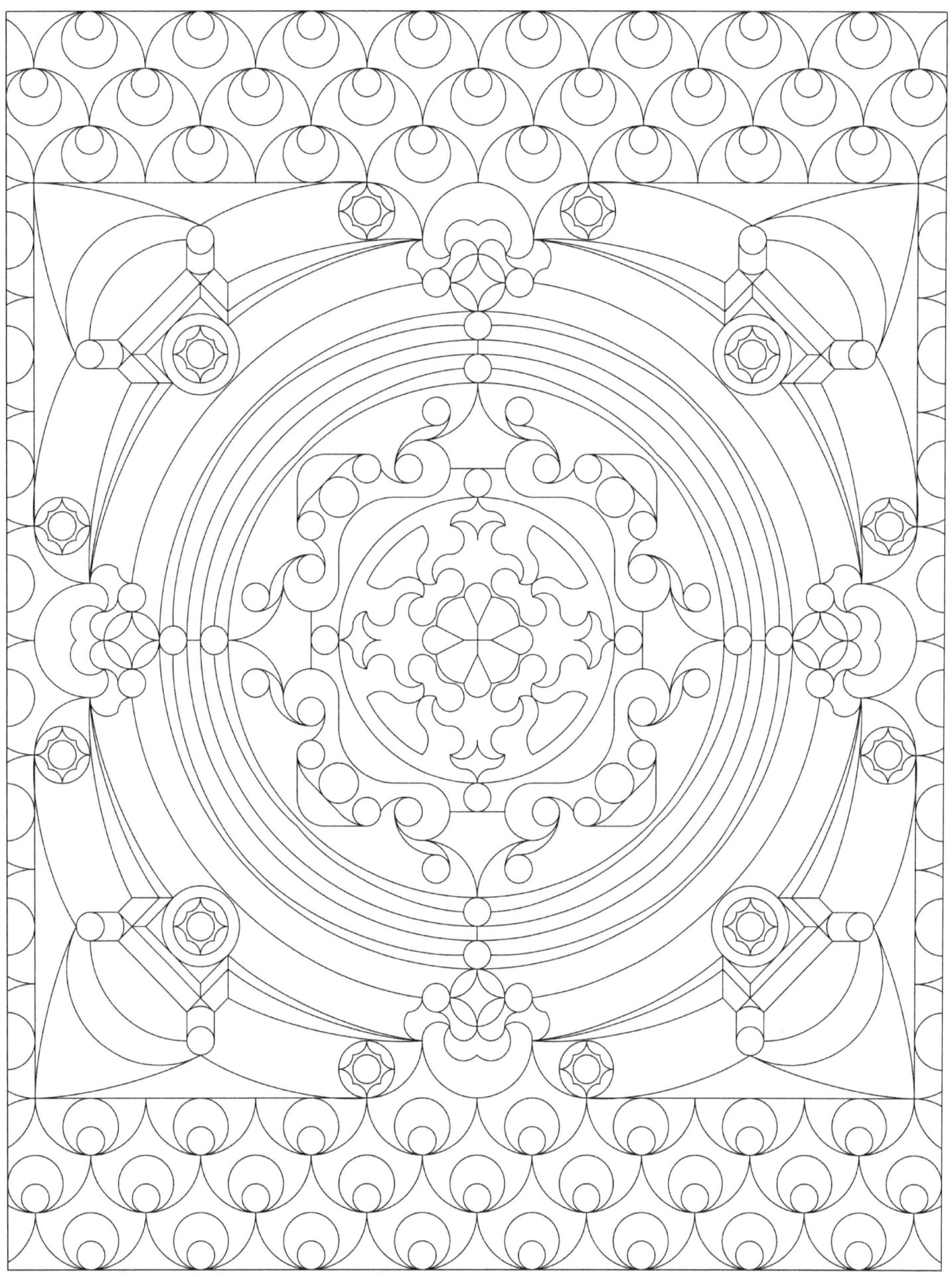

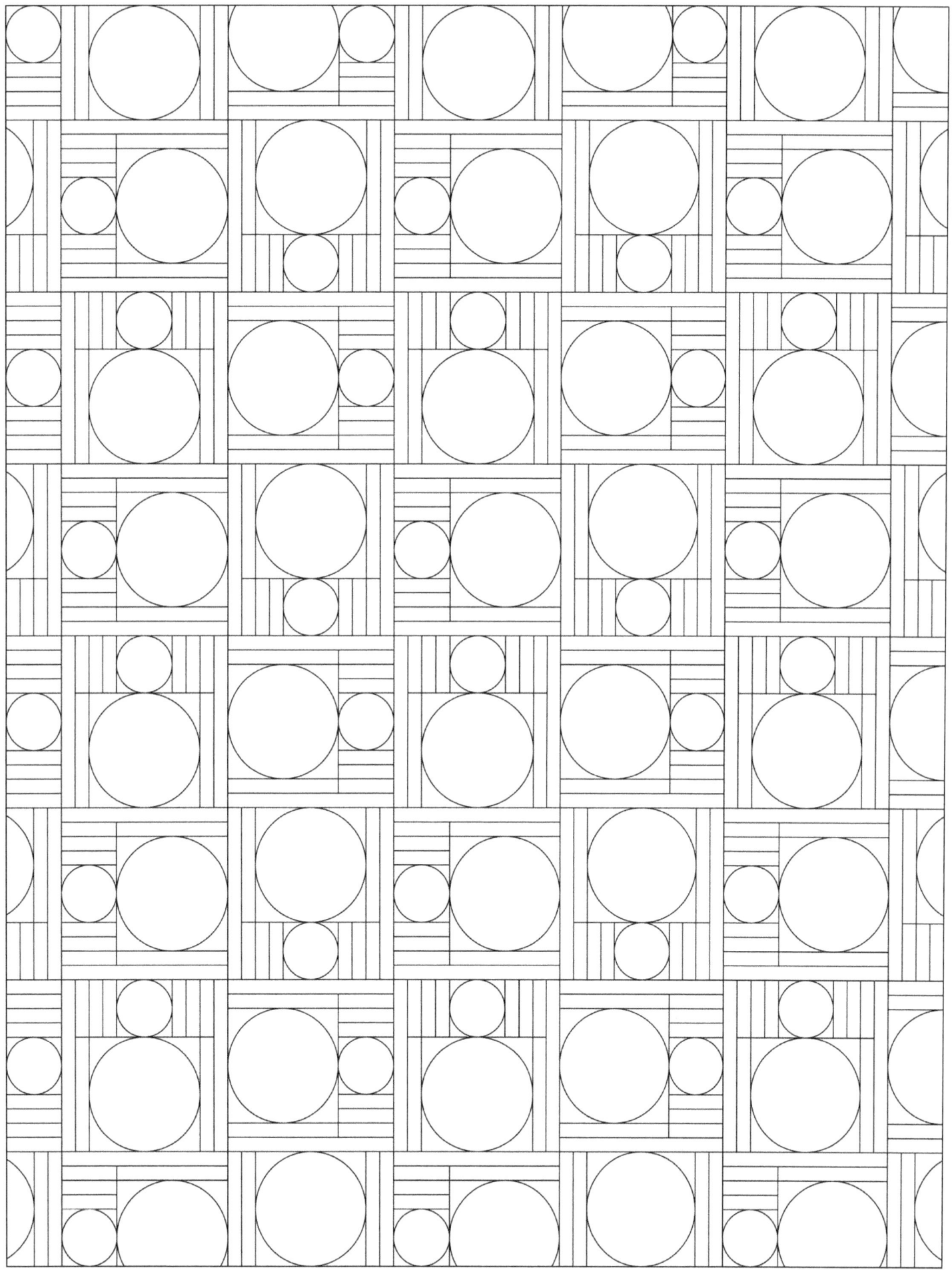

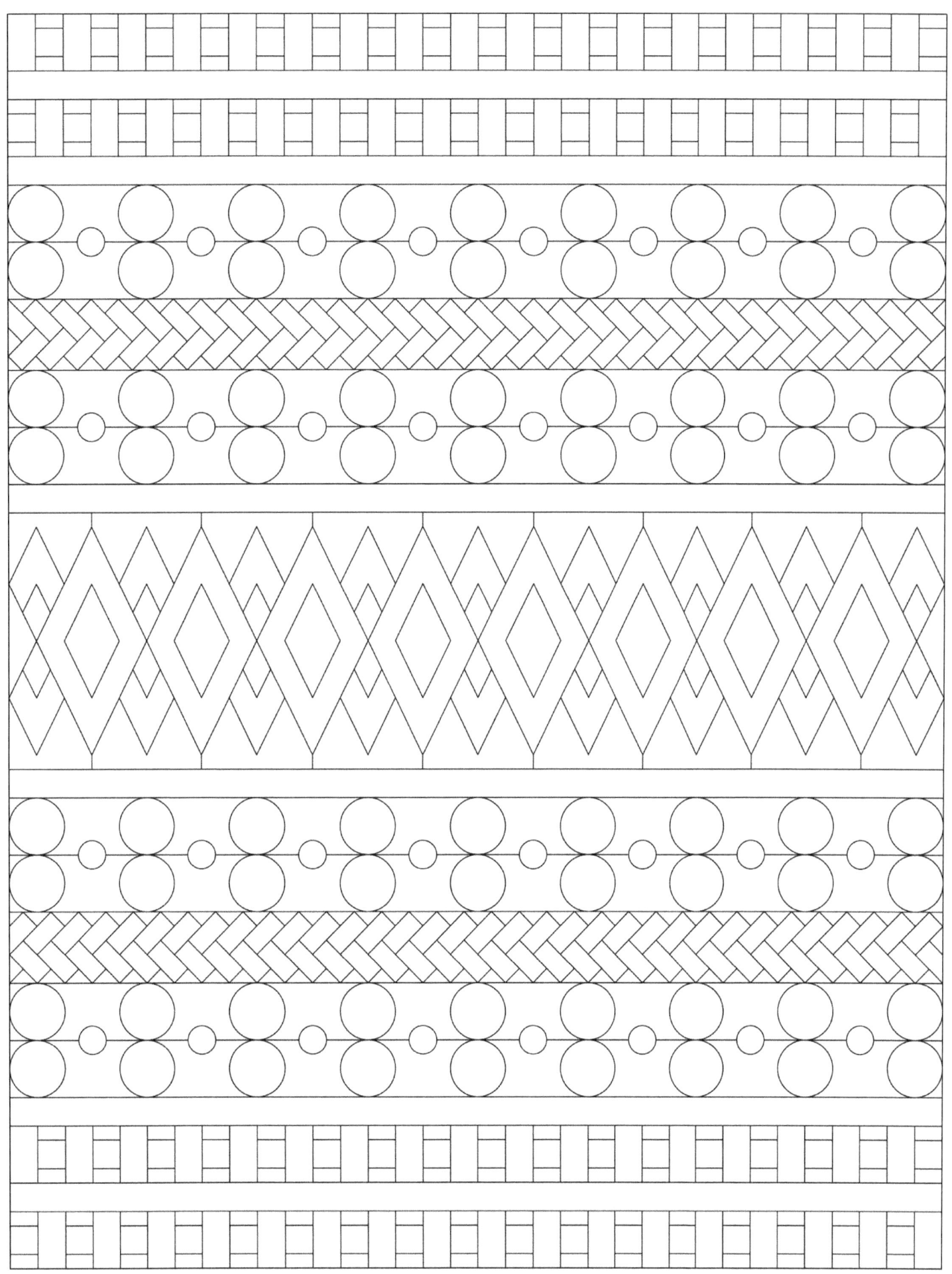

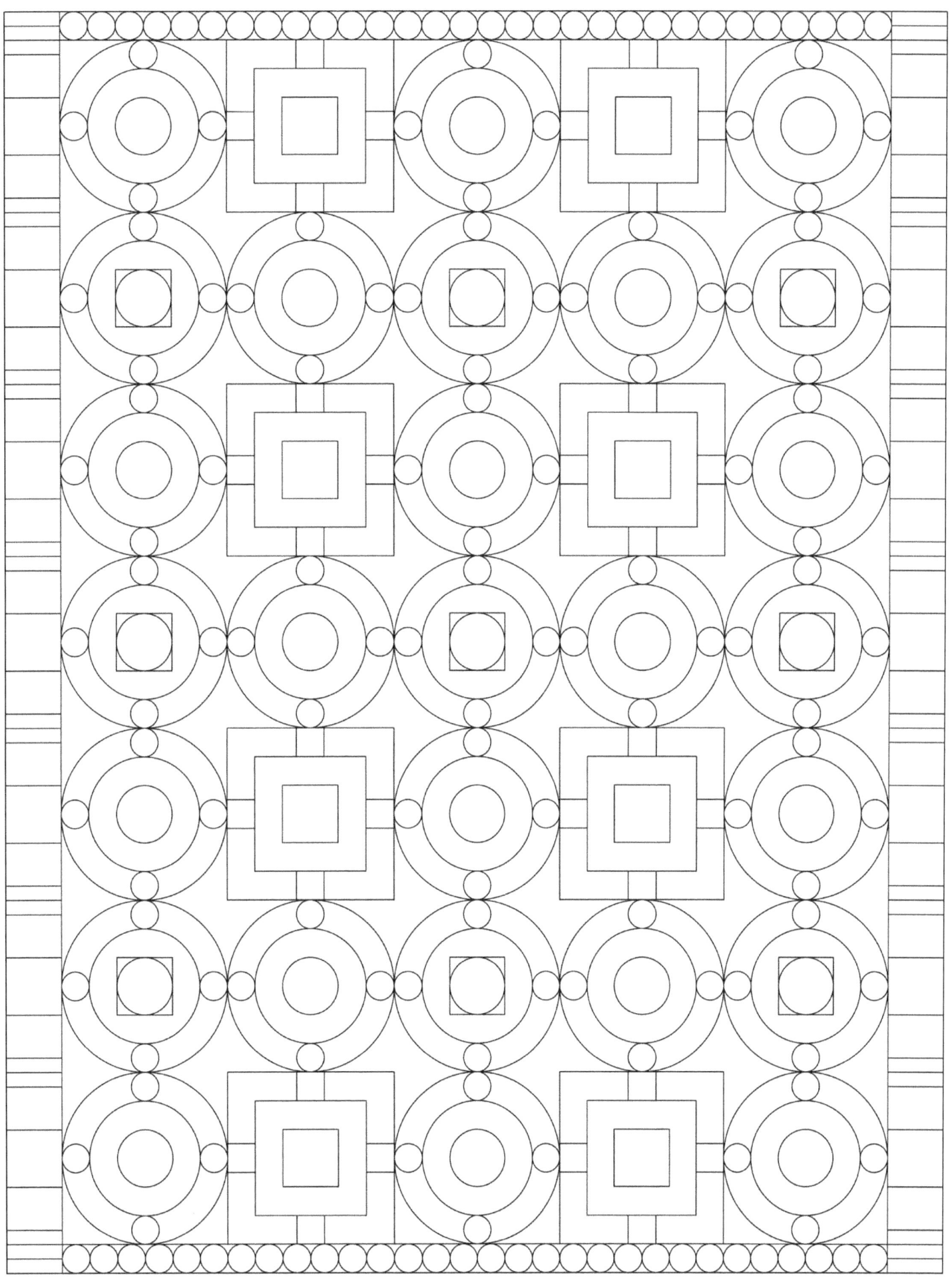

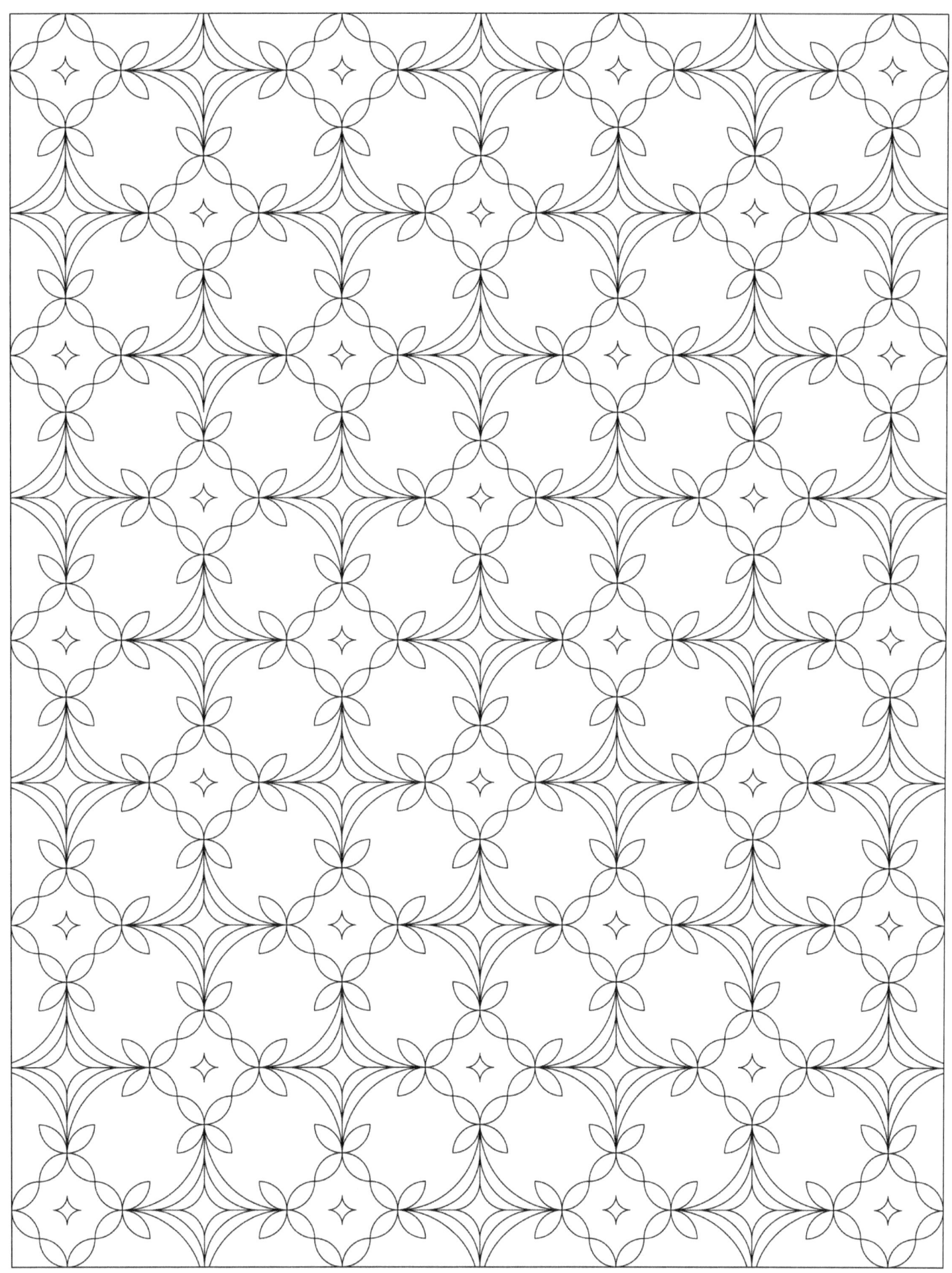

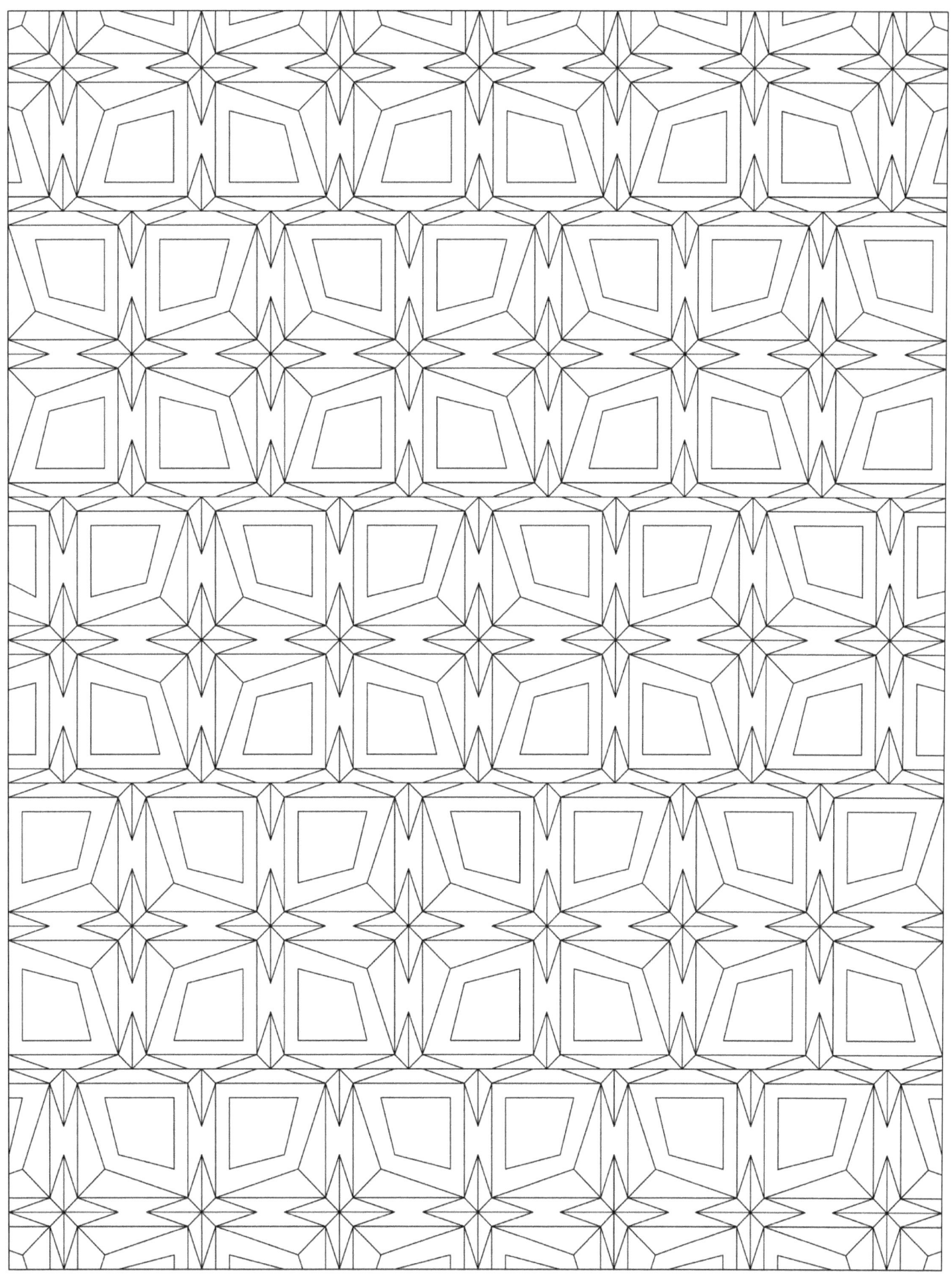

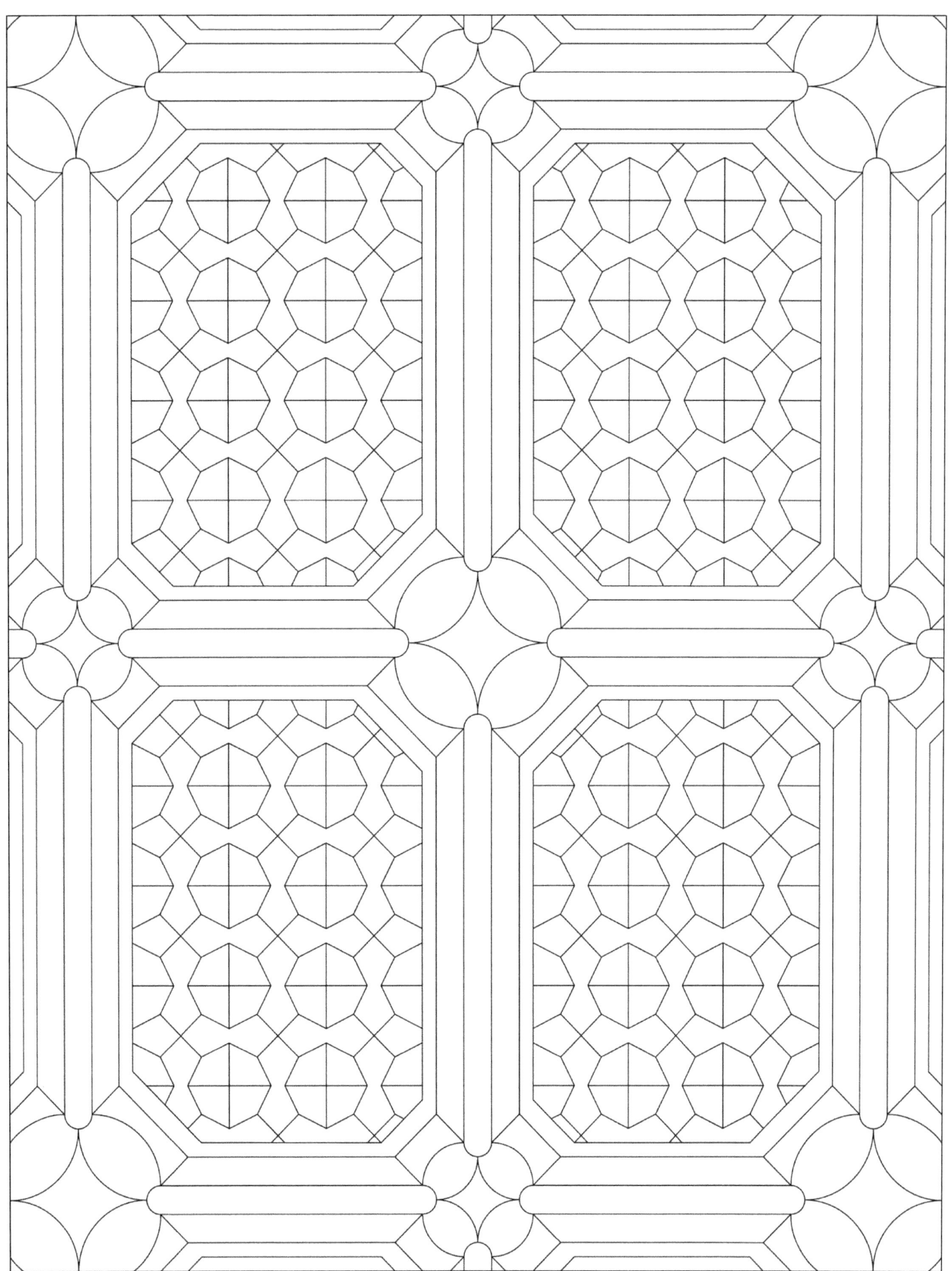

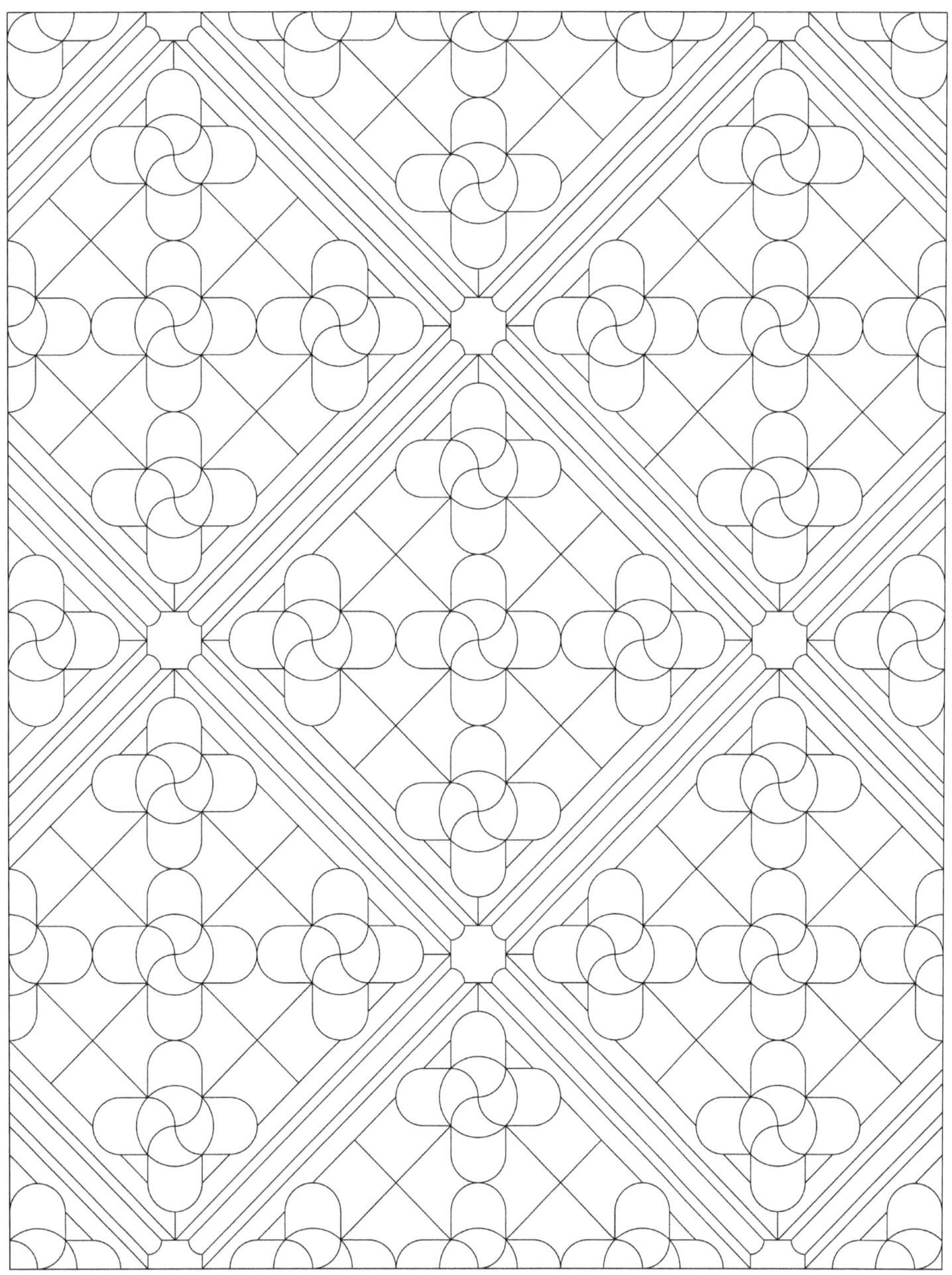

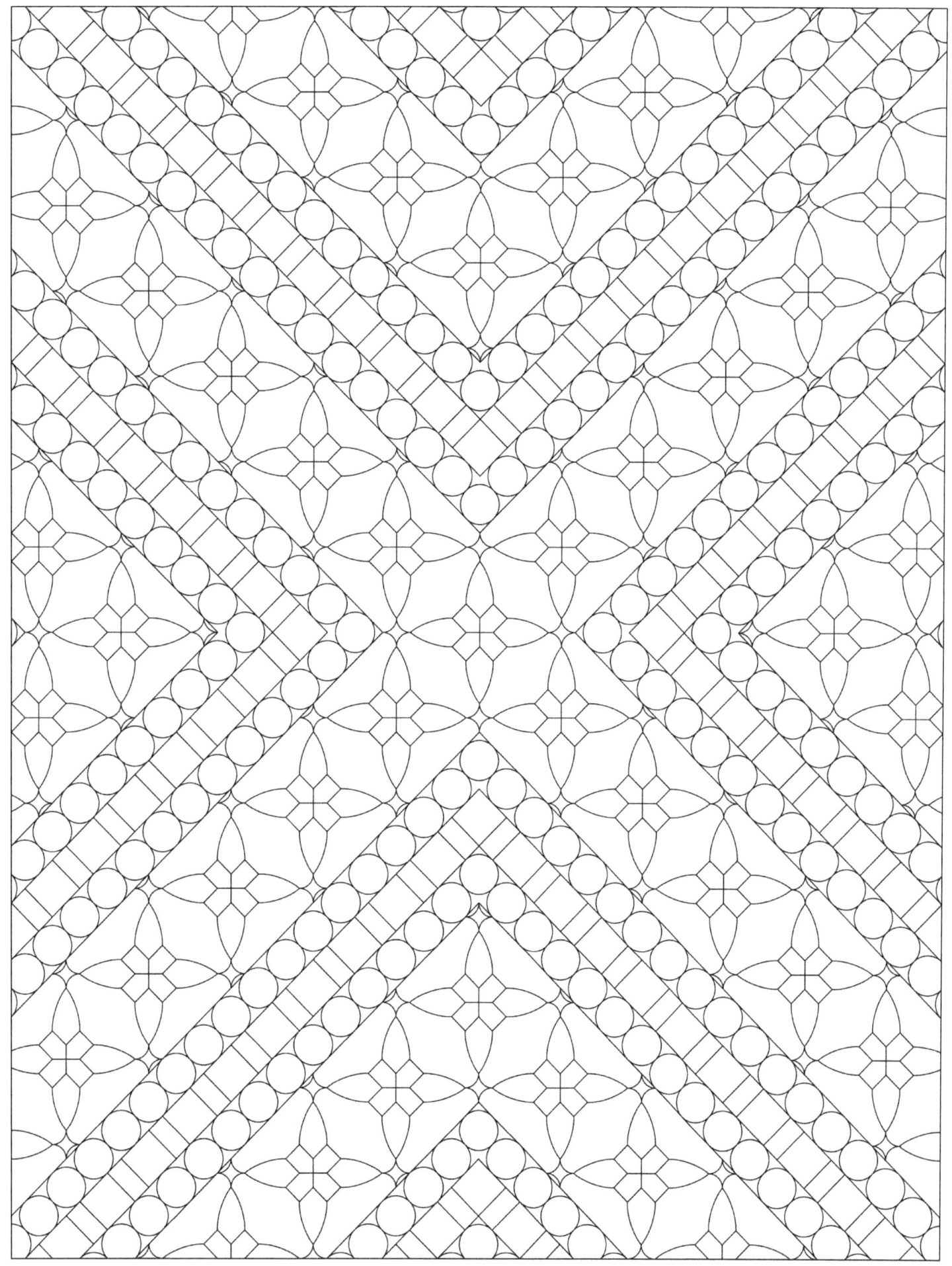

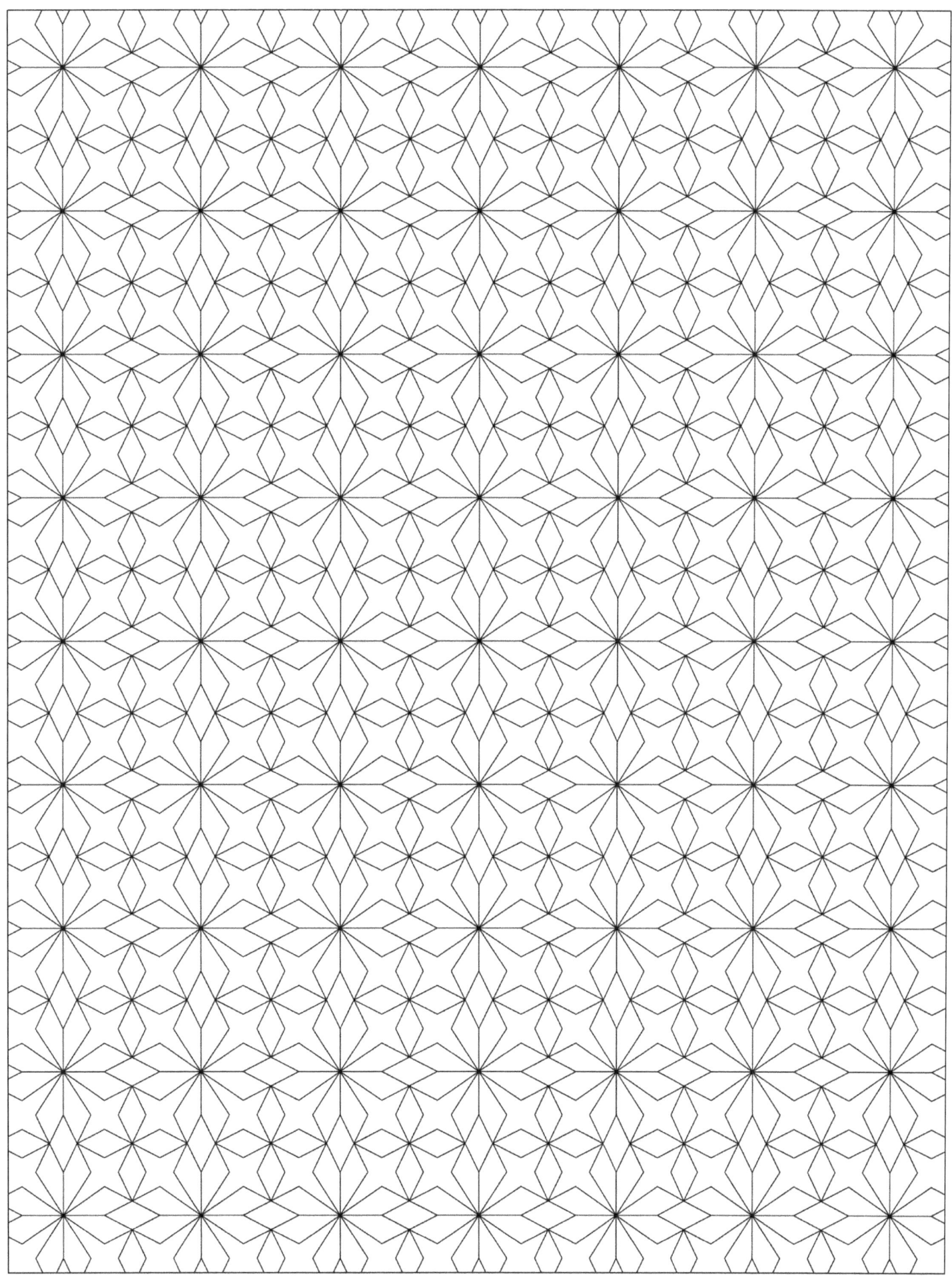

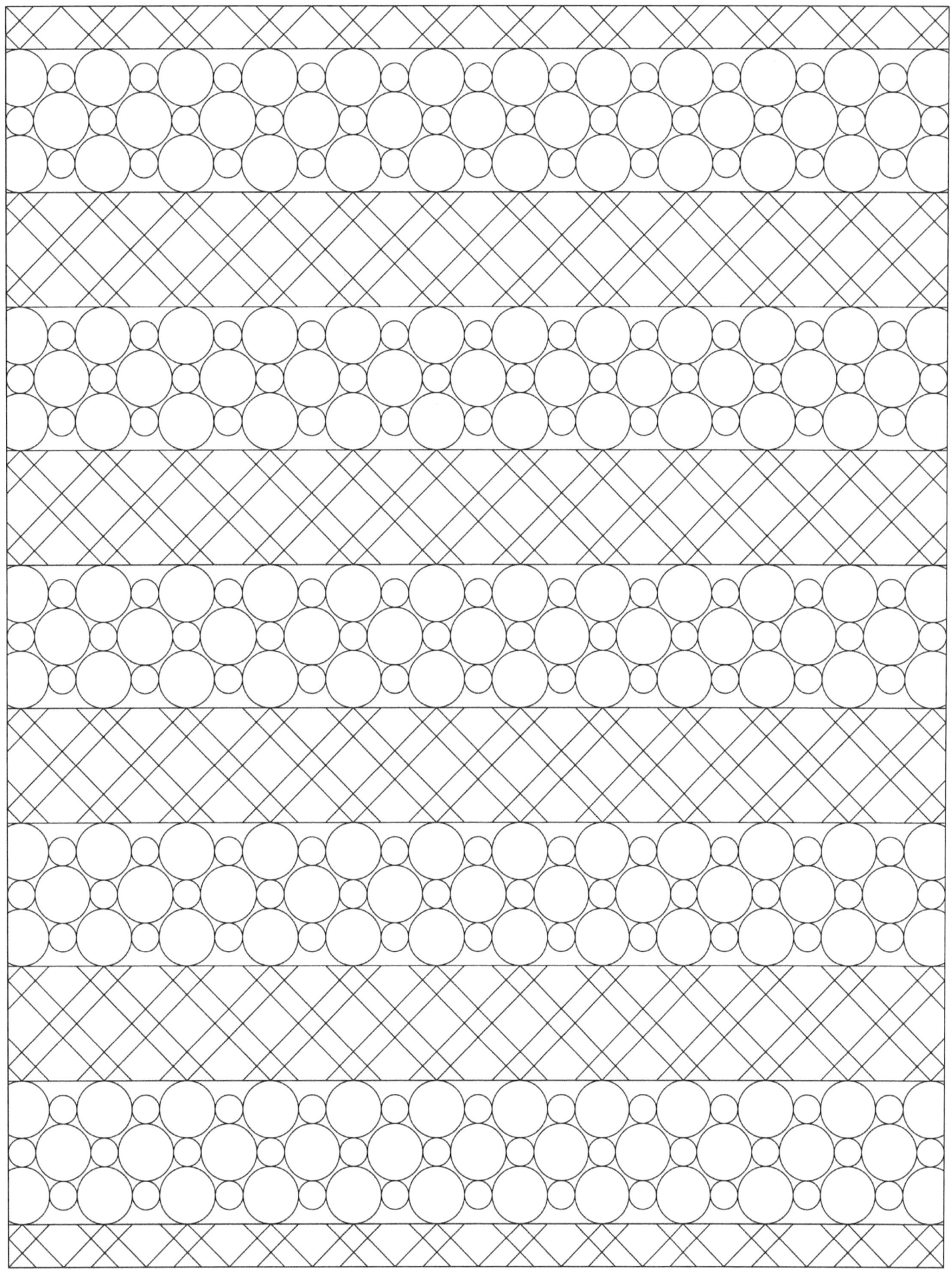

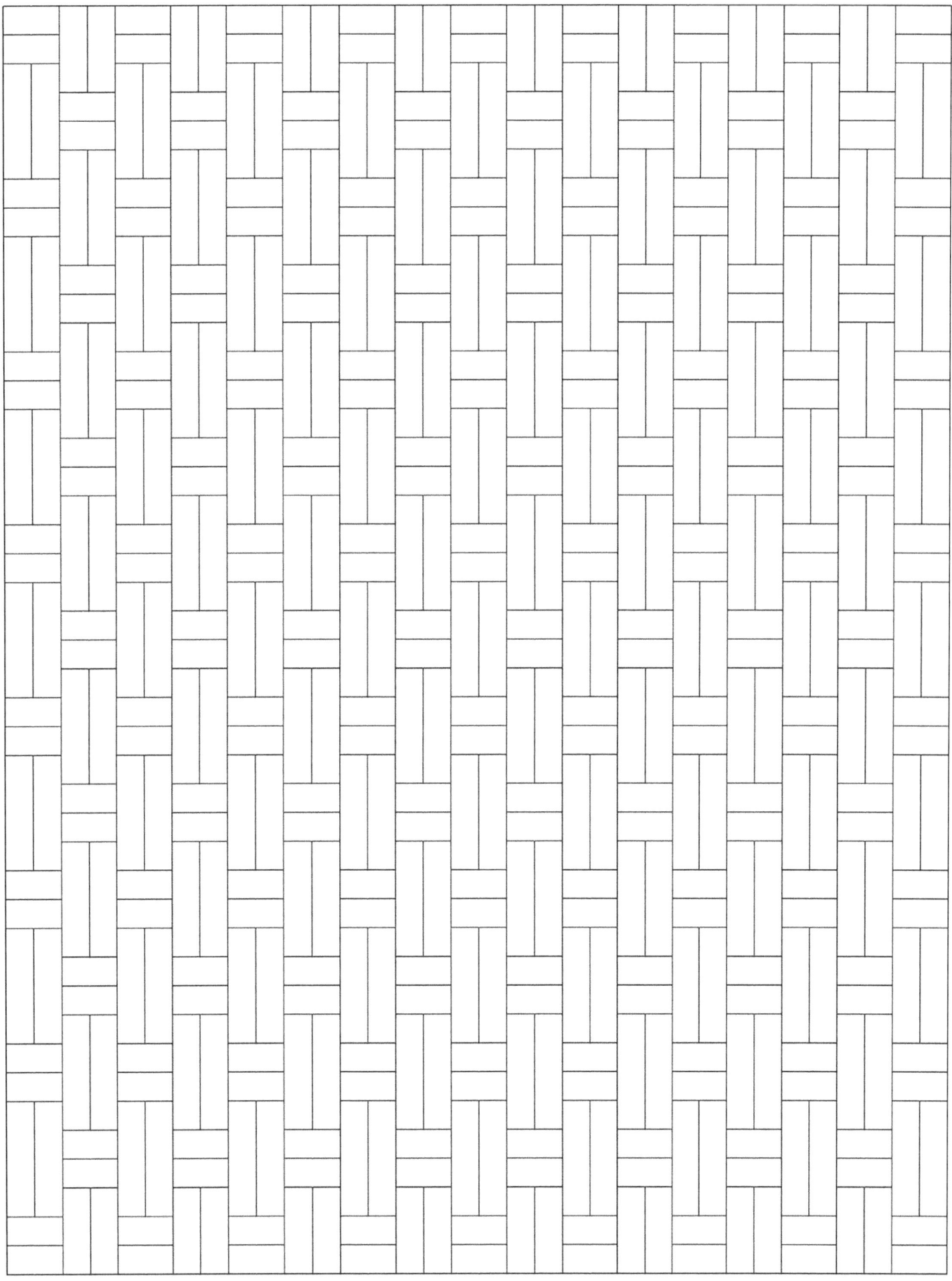

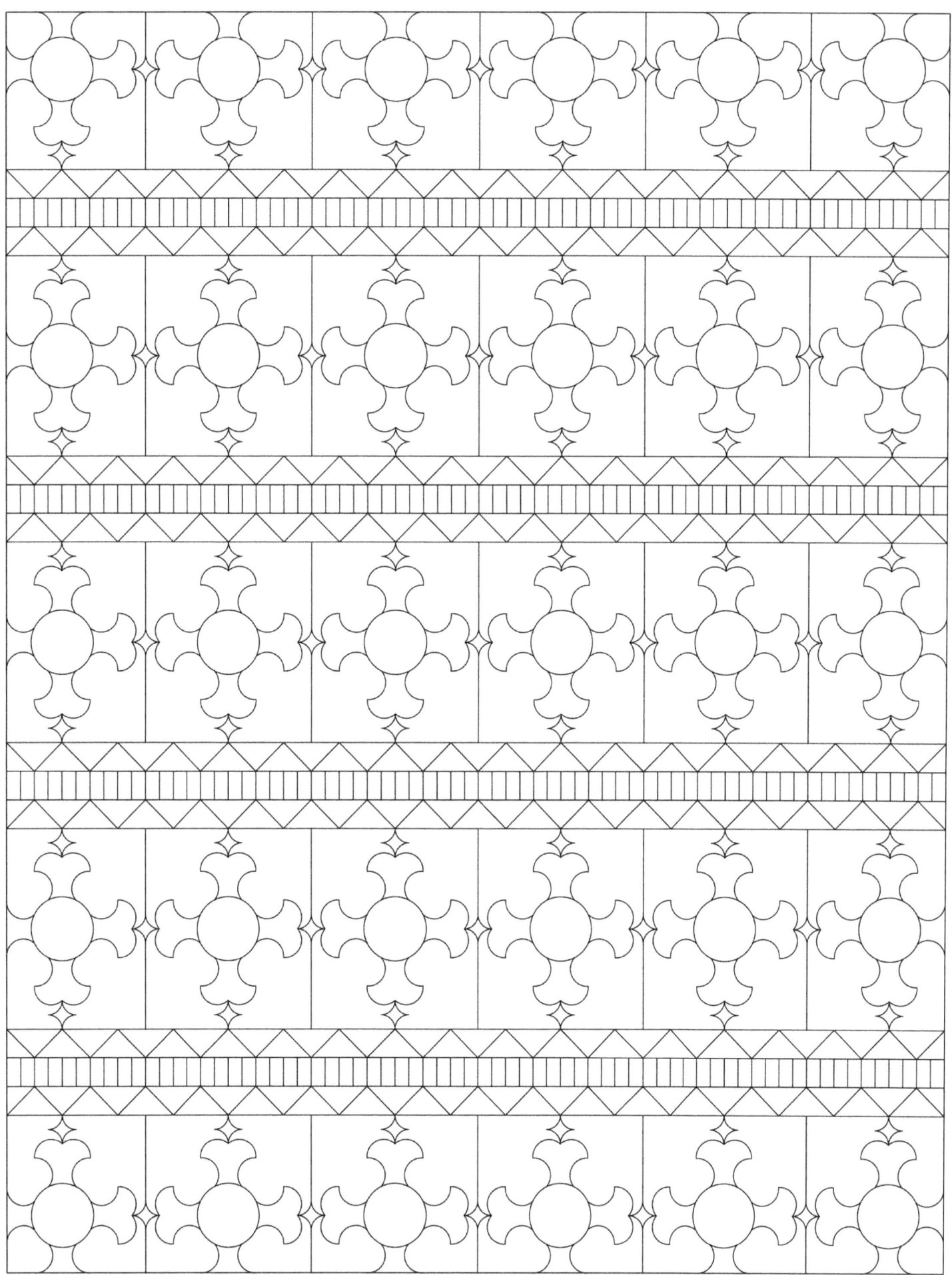

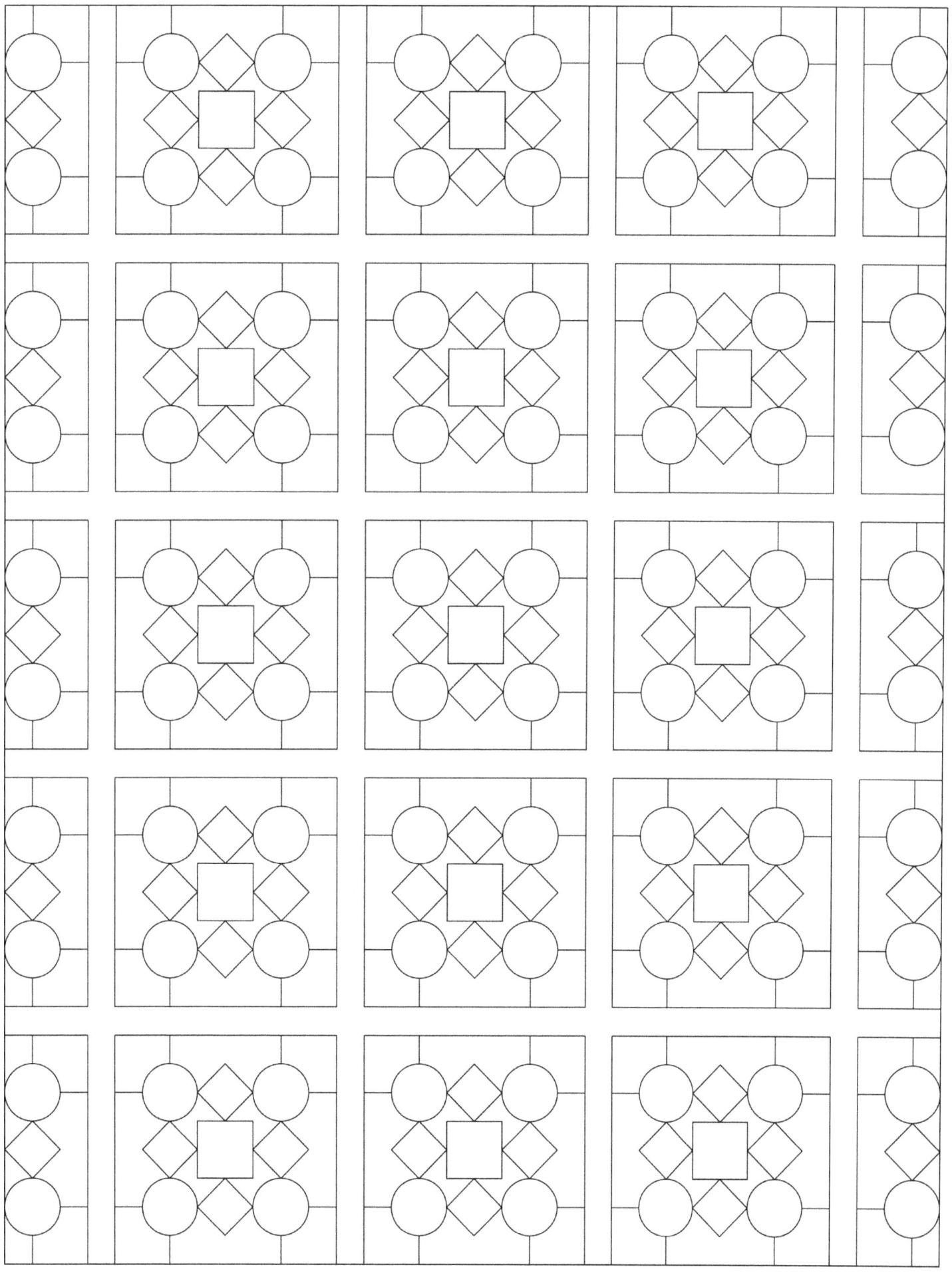

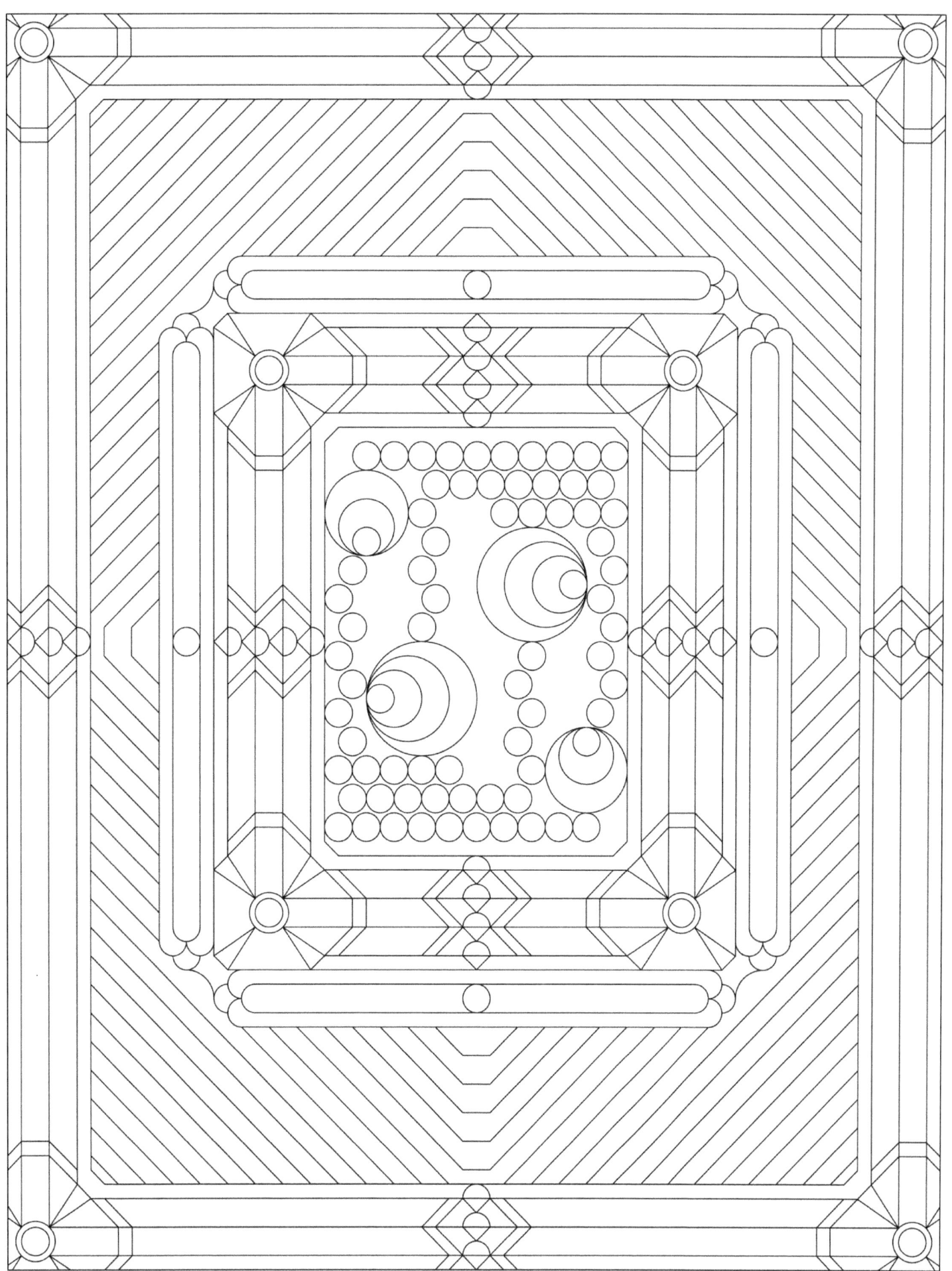

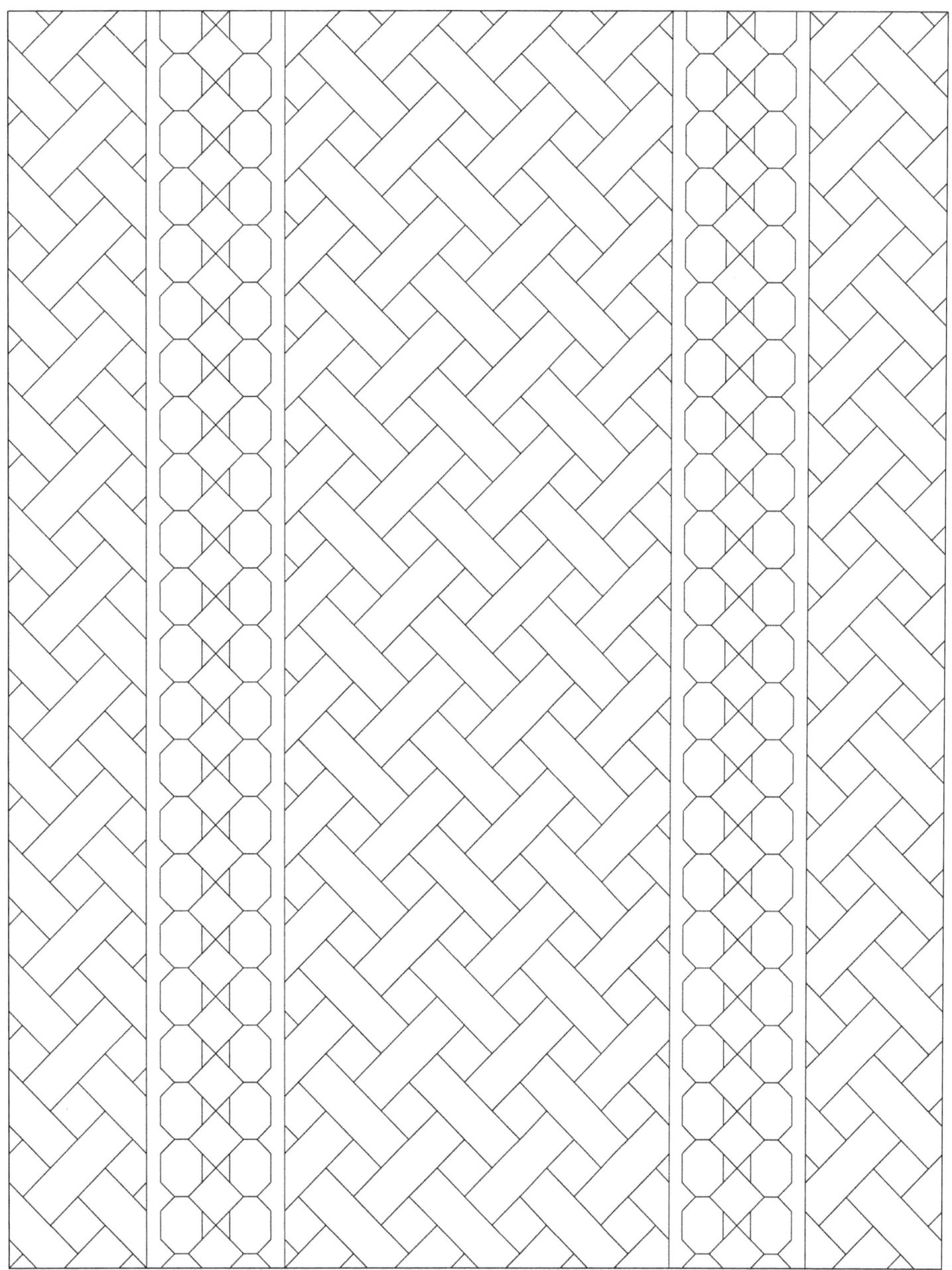

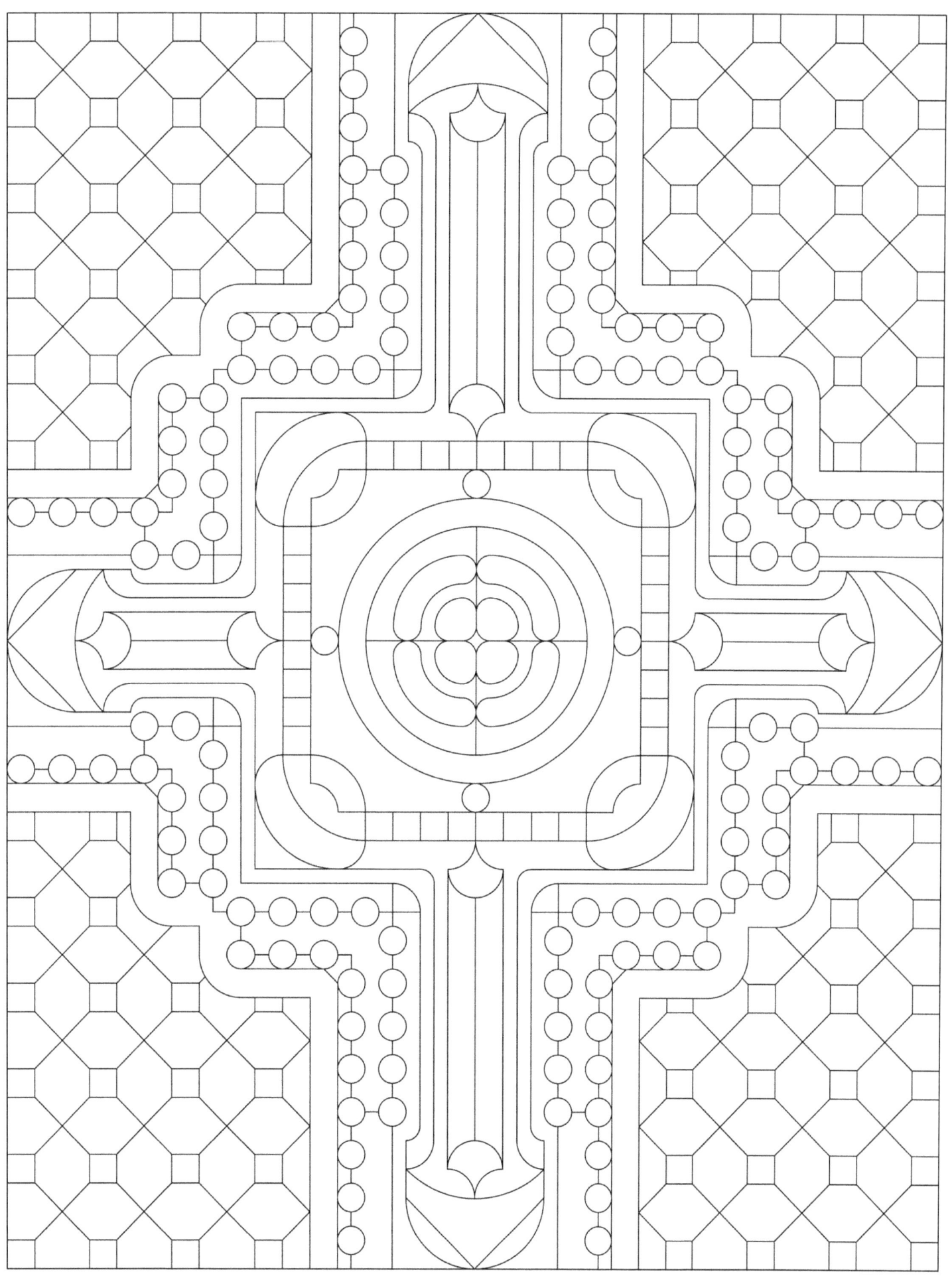

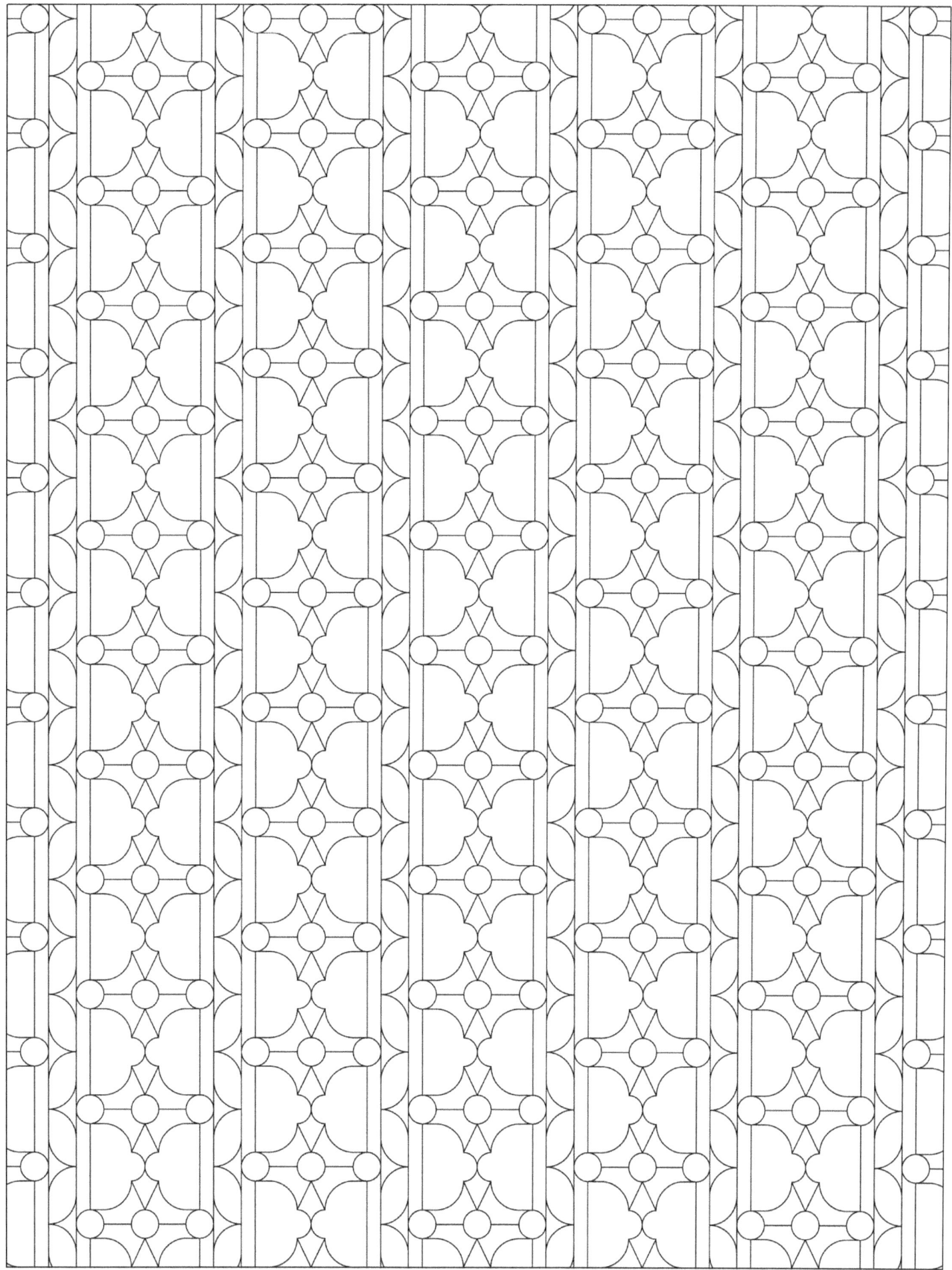

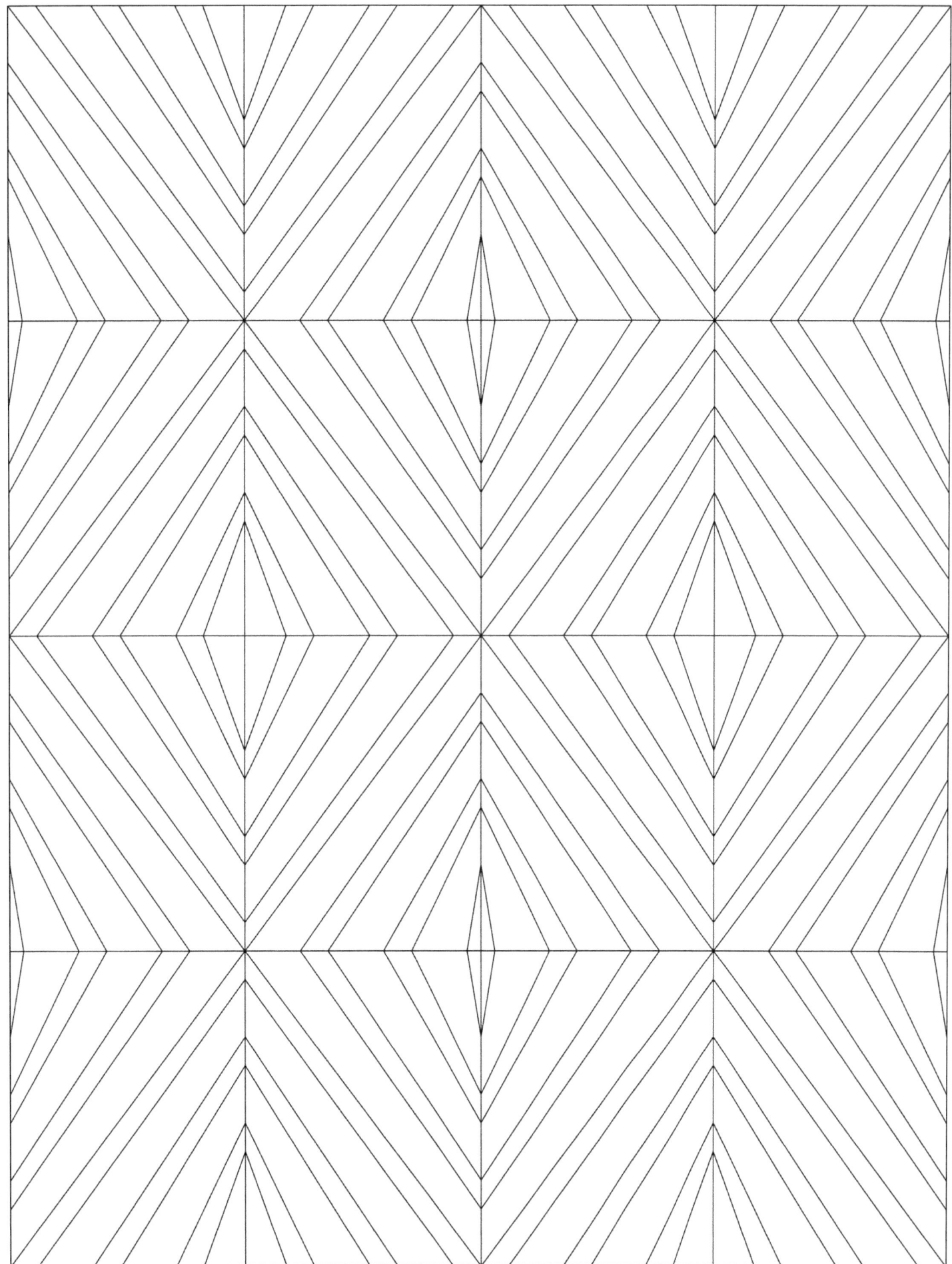

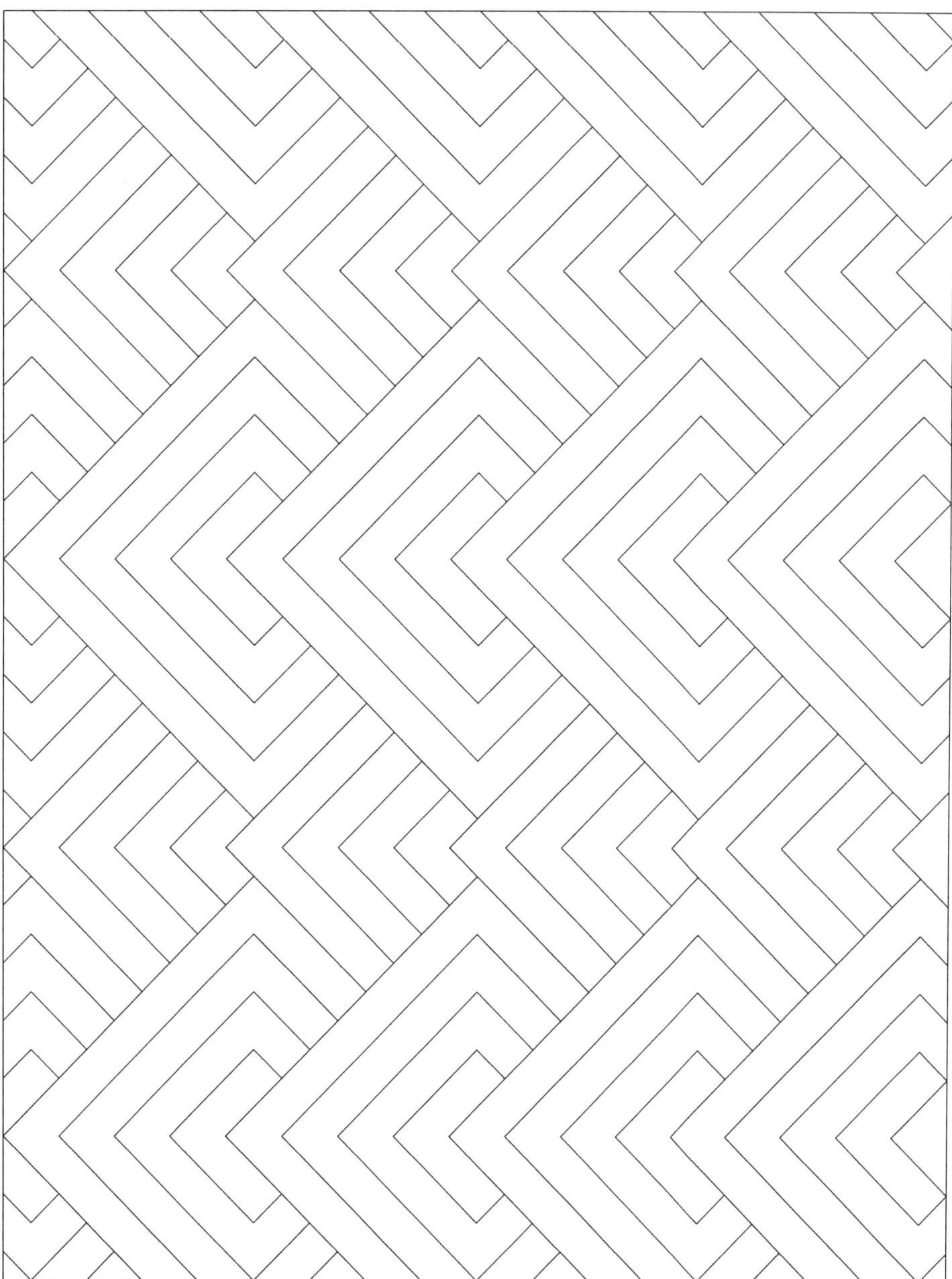

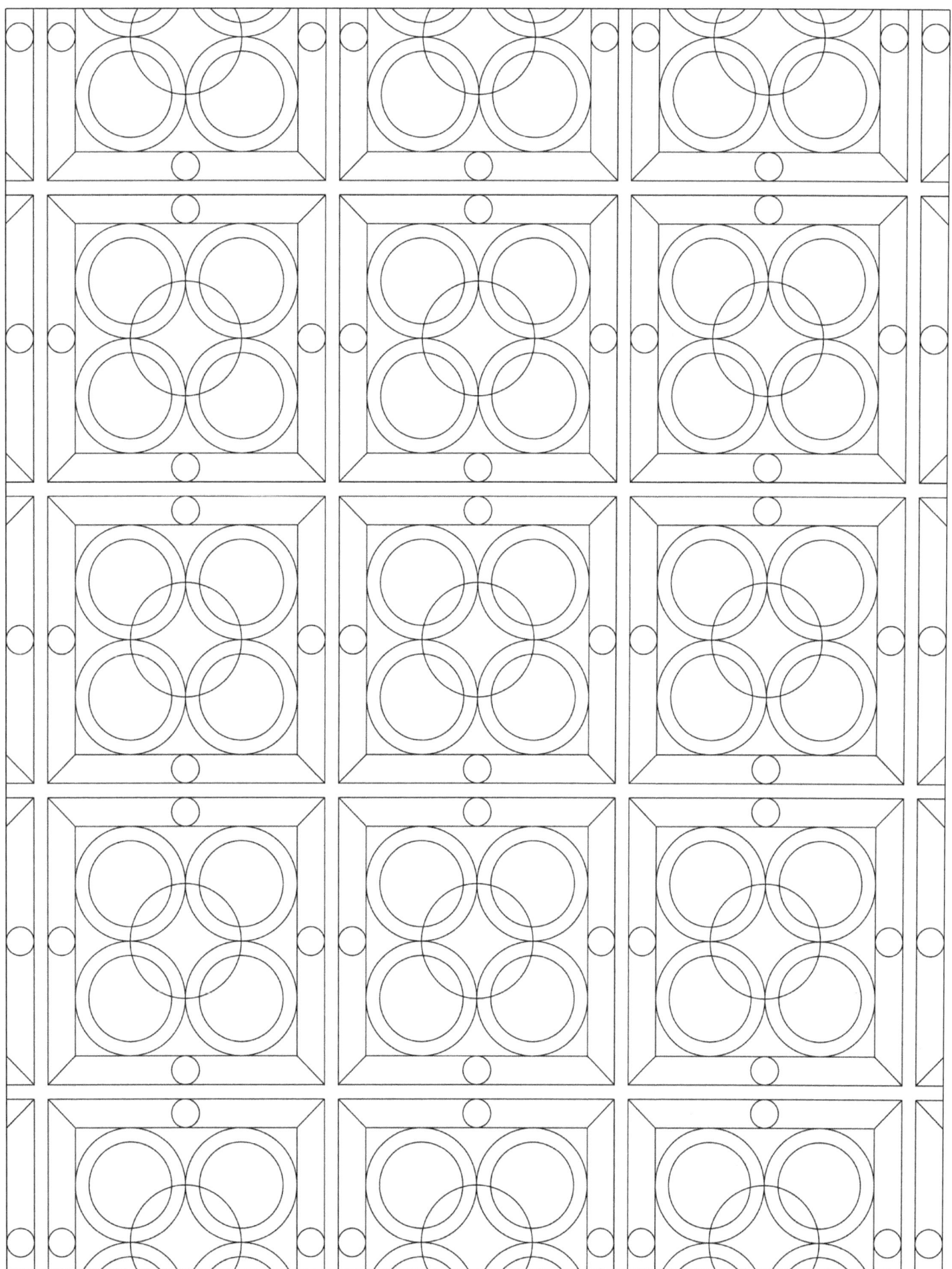

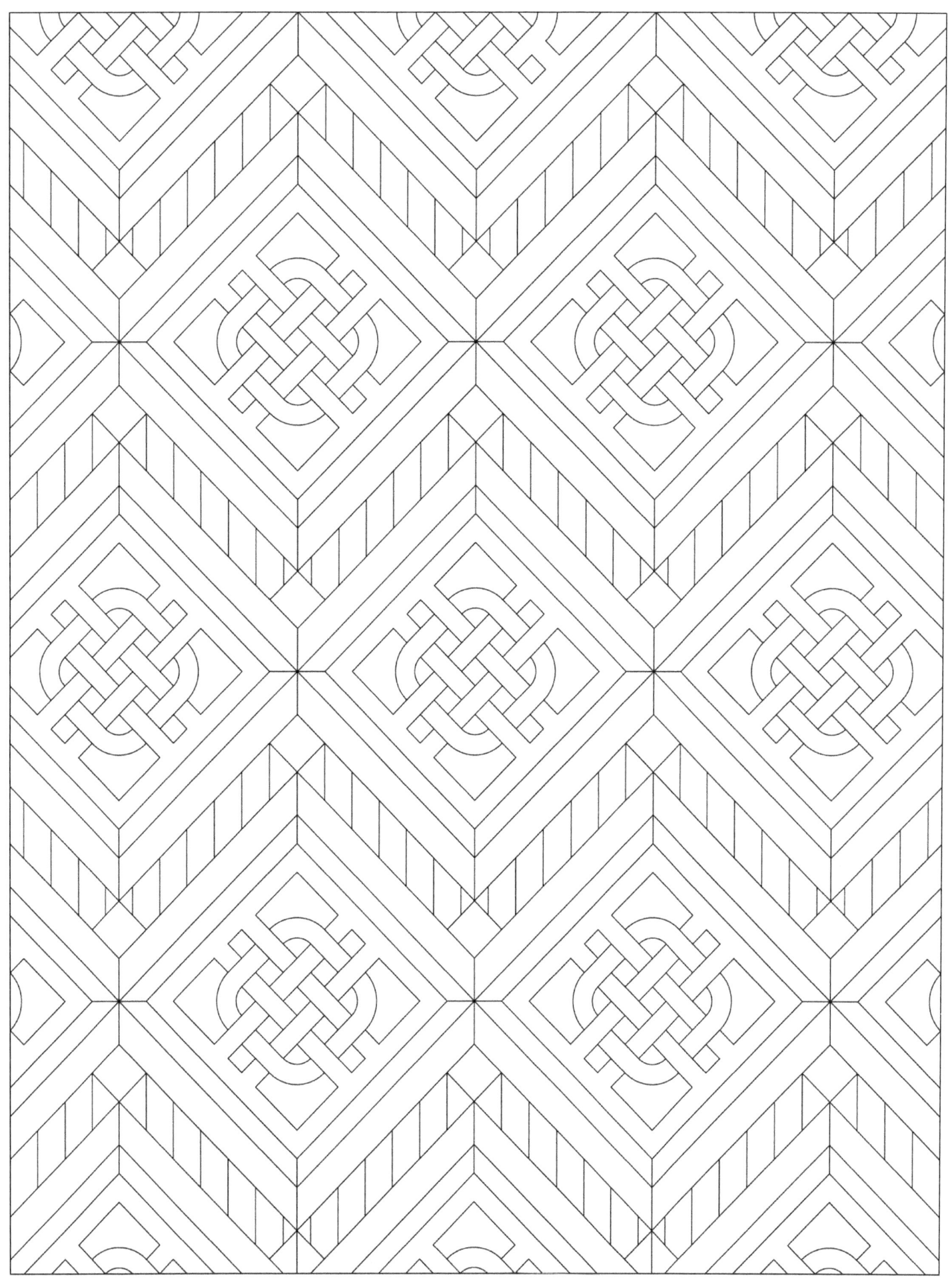

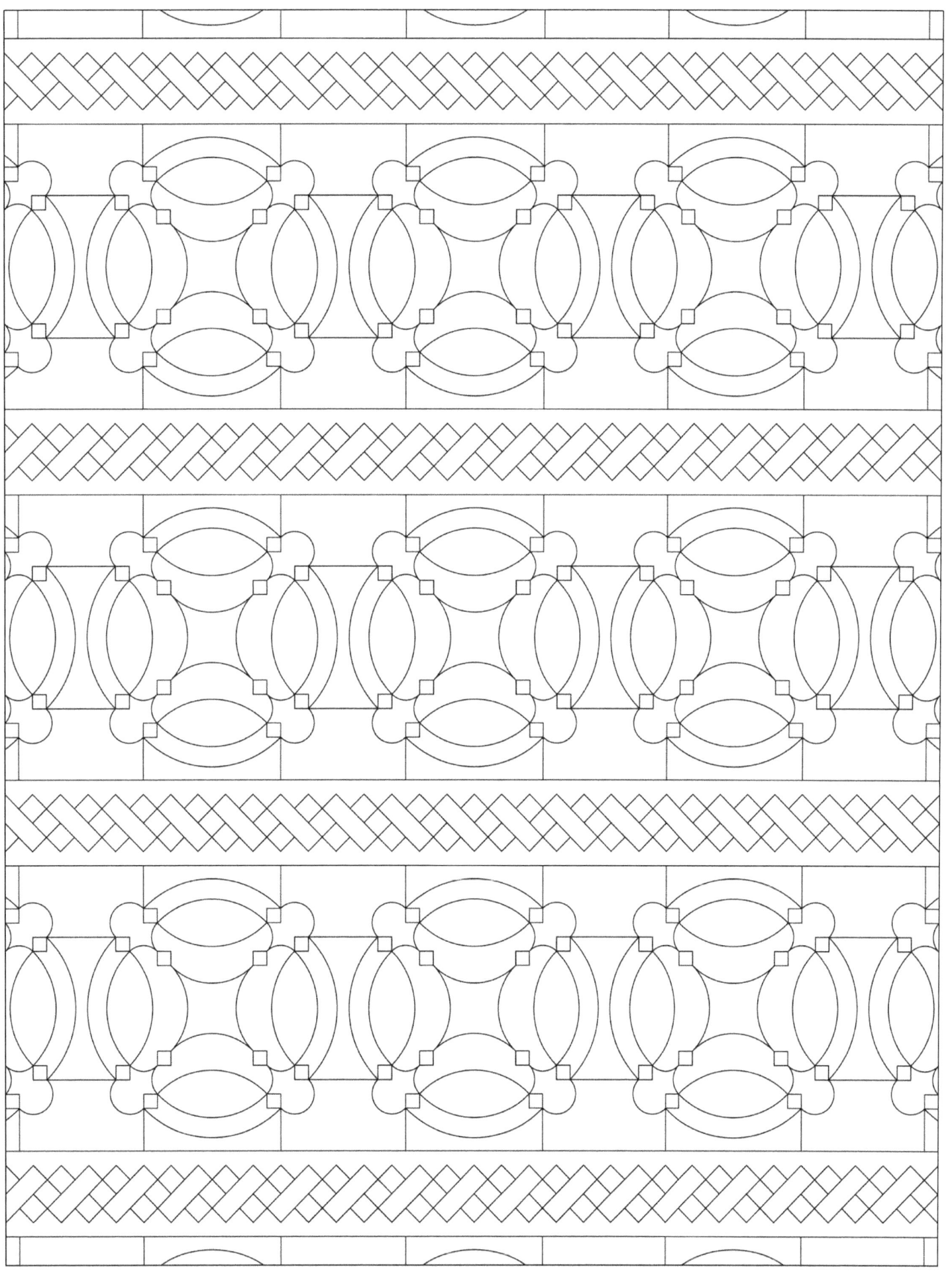

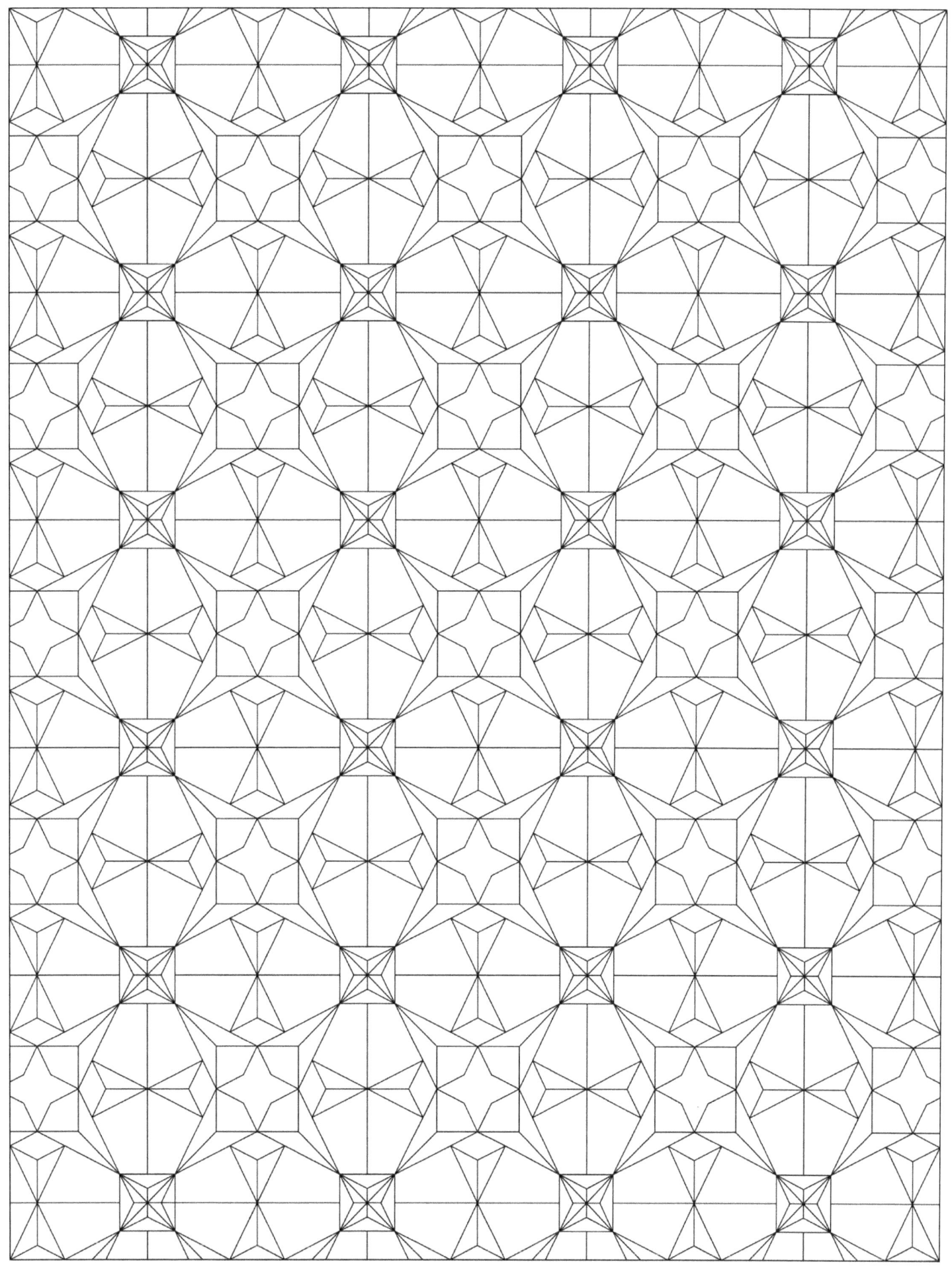

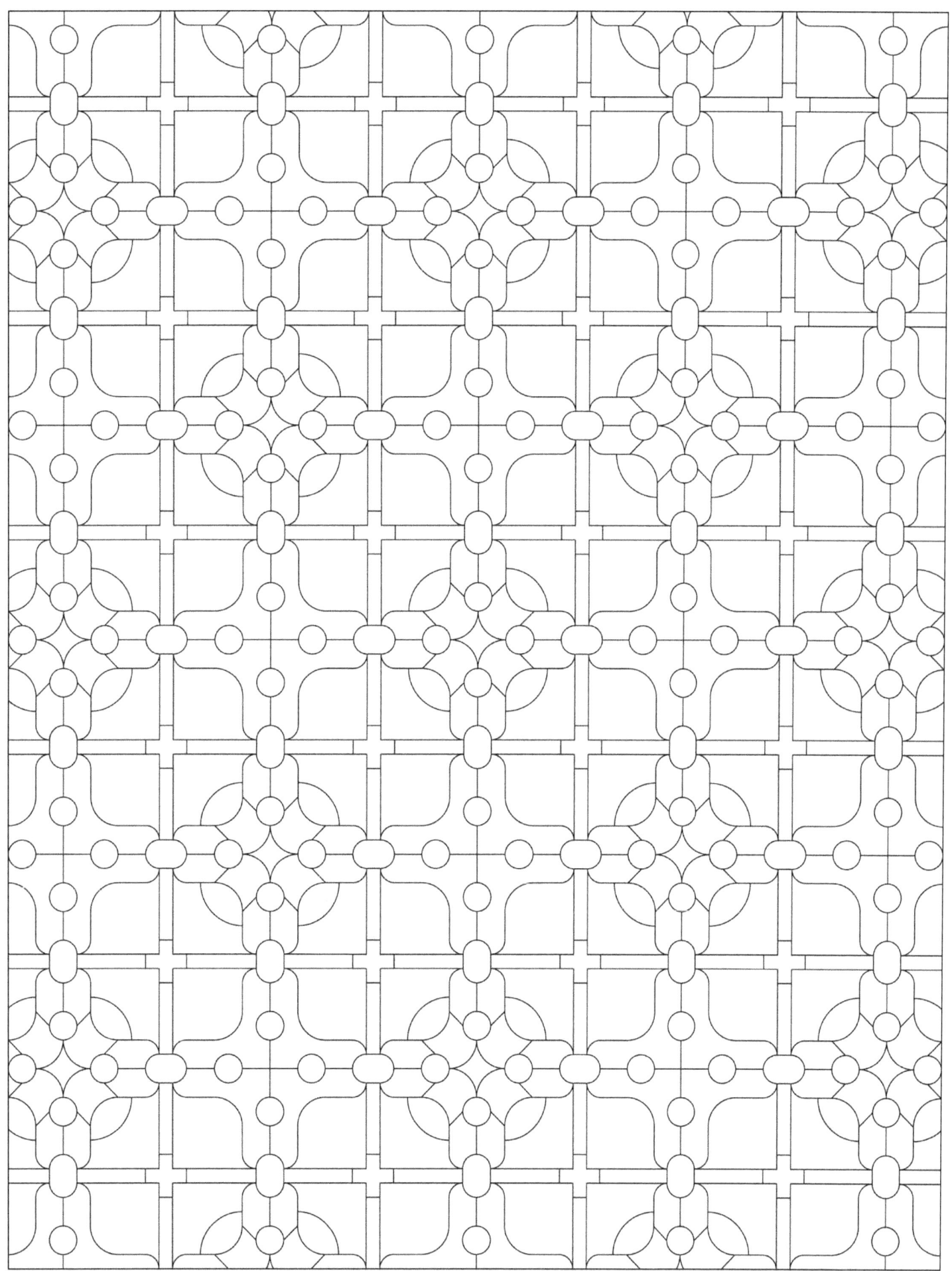

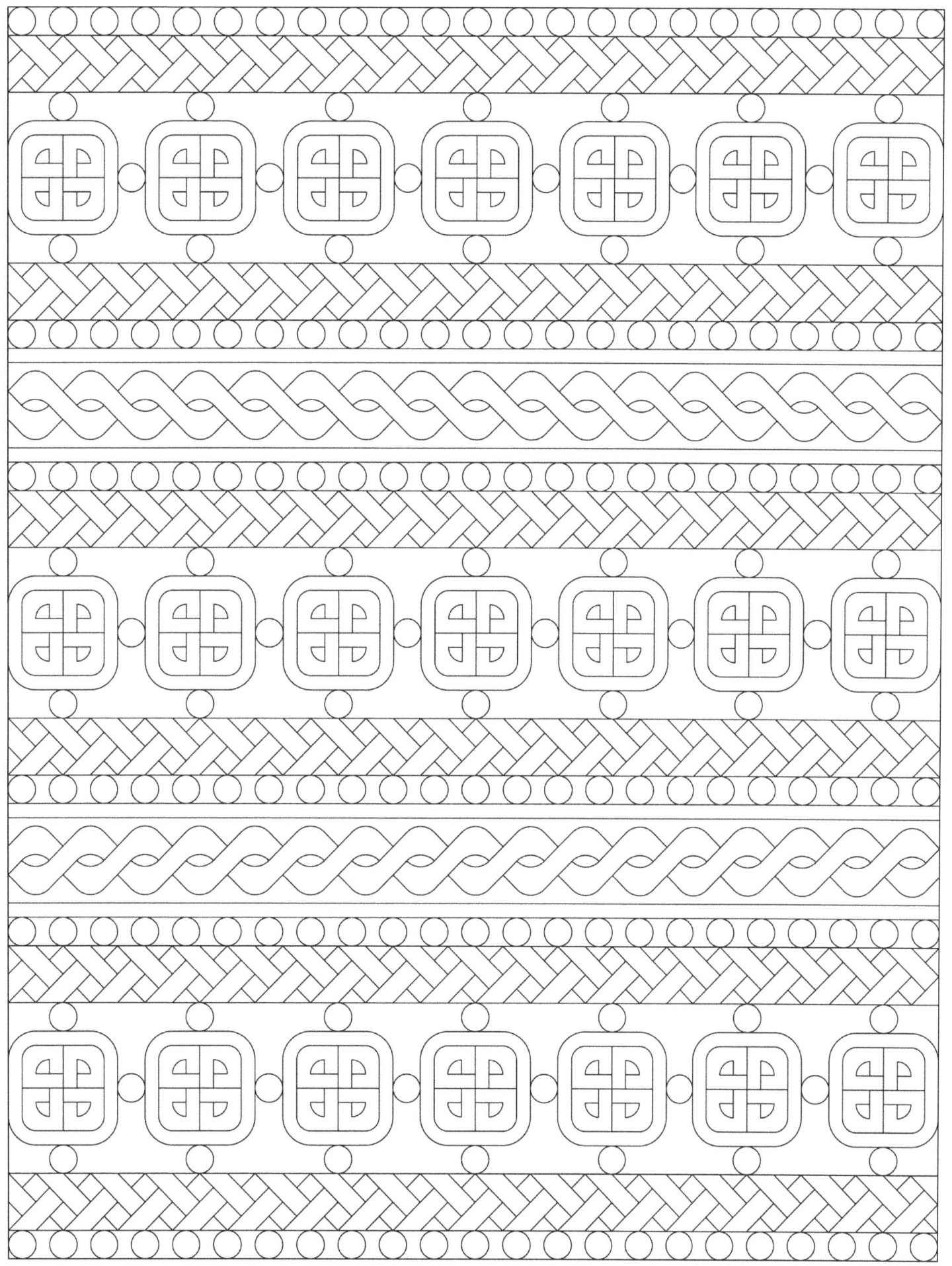